I0762644

SOCCER
SMARTER
FOR KIDS
LEARN TO PLAY
LIKE THE PROS
ANDREW
LATHAM

callisto
publishing
an imprint of Sourcebooks

Callisto Kids,
An imprint of Callisto Publishing LLC

Published by Callisto Publishing LLC C/O Sourcebooks LLC
P.O. Box 4410, Naperville, Illinois 60567-4410
(630) 961-3900
callistopublishing.com

Text by Andrew Latham
Cover Designer: Will Mack

Art Director: Lisa Schreiber
Art Producer: Stacey Stambaugh
Editor: Pamela Bobowicz
Production Editor: Rachel Taenzler
Production Designer: Jeffrey Piekarz

The authorized representative in the EU for product safety and compliance is Dorling Kindersley, Verlag GmbH., Arnulfstr. 124, 80636 Munich, Germany.

Cataloging-in-Publication Data is on file with the Library of Congress.

Source of Production: Versa Press
Date of production: January 2026
Run Number: 5054912

Printed in the United States of America
VP 10 9 8 7 6 5 4 3 2 1

This book is dedicated to every player and coach I have had the fortune to work with. You made me a better coach, and I am grateful for that.

SOCCER
GOAL
#1

TABLE OF CONTENTS

Introduction

What do all soccer legends have in common? What links Cristiano Ronaldo and Lionel Messi, Abby Wambach and Mia Hamm, David Beckham and Alex Morgan? The answer is they all played soccer as kids. That makes these professional players the same as you. You share your passion for soccer with them.

This book is aimed at kids who have been playing soccer for a while, have a good understanding of the basics of the game, and want to kick their skills up a notch. Does that sound like you? If so, you are in the right place.

My name is Andrew Latham, and I have been playing and coaching soccer most of life. My focus throughout may surprise you: It's not to win games. It's always to help players improve. We know that soccer is a team sport. But within that, there are many individual battles that take place all over the field—the battles of each player. The goal of this book is to help you win *your* battles, and in turn, help your team win the game!

In the first section of this book we will look at how you can prepare for your success on the field with some things that you can do away from the field. Things like planning your nutrition, managing your time, and getting enough rest.

In part two we will focus on techniques. In soccer, *technique* is all about being consistent and efficient with the ball. We'll look at a variety of techniques for all positions except for goalkeeper, as that role has a unique set of skills. Very often we practice technique in an unopposed situation. But what is an opponent? It's not always a player; it can be time, space, or even the environment we are playing in, like wind or sleet. The more often we practice a technique, against as many "opponents" as possible, the more it becomes a skill. There is no skill without the practice of technique. Even natural skill needs practice.

In the third part of the book, we will focus on strategies that will help take your game to the next level. *Strategy* is all about the plan, and your role within that plan. A lot of strategy is based around decision-making and how you react to the decisions made by the player with the ball—whether that is a teammate or an opponent. Soccer is like chess, because there are an almost infinite number of moves and game plays, it's hard to predict what will happen, and it has lots of moving parts.

In the final section of the book, part four, we will talk about how to prepare for the move to the full-field game. We'll look at new formations and some other parts of the game that you may not have had to think about when playing on a smaller field. Throughout the book, I will try to link some of the sections together to help make things a little clearer. And for each technique, strategy, or skill, I'll mention the name of a professional player, team, or game to watch that demonstrates a particular thing really well. Watching other players practice and perform a skill will help you practice your technique. Doing some research yourself will help you understand more about soccer as a game and becoming a better player.

I hope you'll take some of the techniques in this book and make them part of your regular individual practice. I also hope you change these techniques as you grow, making them more challenging as you improve. The pro players featured in this book all have talent, but what separates them from everyone else is that they have desire and a first-class work ethic. Work hard, and maybe you too will be featured in a book like this someday!

You can read this book cover to cover like a novel or pick and choose sections as needed. It's your book; read it any way you'd like—just be sure to read it, and practice the techniques if you want to see any benefits!

It's time to kick off. Let's go!

PART 1

Preparing for Success

Being a good soccer player is about more than being good at soccer on the field.

In this section I will talk about the things you can do off the field that will be important to your success as you move through the developmental age group levels. If you want to play in college and then have a professional career, the tips in this section will help you achieve that. Not only that, but as you get older, nutrition, rest, physical conditioning, your behavior off the field, and your mental health become bigger factors in any success that you will have. And if you want to continue playing soccer for fun with your friends, then these tips will help you, too. Eating well, staying hydrated, learning how to make a plan, and staying in shape will also improve many other parts of your life! By making good habits now, you are setting yourself up for success later.

Your Integrated Support Team

At the highest levels of the sport—the Olympics and the World Cup—soccer players work with members of what we call an **Integrated Support Team** or **IST**. While the coaches work on soccer skills and techniques to perform in a game or practice, the IST works on things like nutrition, strength and conditioning, recovery, physiology (which means how the body works), and mental performance.

The team that you play for now probably doesn't have a support team like the IST. But *you* have a support team—your parents or guardians.

Your parents have watched you play, driven you to practice, and won and lost games with you since your first time on the field. You can go to them when you want to think about your individual game. If you need help learning a skill, communicating with a teammate or coach, or setting a path forward for your success, your IST can help.

But some other things that are important to your success as a player are your nutrition and your time management. Your IST can help you with these, too.

What you eat and drink, and more importantly what you *don't* eat and drink, will play a big part in your success on the field. Working with your parents on making a weekly diet and understanding some basic nutritional tips will keep you healthy and fueled up. It might also help them, too!

Something else your parents can help you with is goal setting. Success doesn't happen overnight no matter how old you are, and it is usually supported by a team behind the team. Asking your parents to be the team behind you—your IST—will put you in a good place to succeed.

Eating to Succeed

In this section, we will look at what to eat, when to eat, how to prepare a personal meal plan, and a little about eating when traveling. I'm not going to tell you what meals to order when you are at dinner or what snacks to eat. I know that we all like and dislike different foods. Think about your nutrition like this: A car needs fuel in order to move. It might be gasoline, or it might be electricity. *You* also need fuel in order to play and train. Your fuel isn't gas or electricity. It's fruit, vegetables, grains, proteins, and dairy.

Every day, try to include vegetables and fruit in your meals and snacks. These foods include nutrients that you need like fiber, vitamins, and minerals. At each meal, try to cover half of your plate with vegetables and fruit! Here are some examples and cheat codes:

1. Look for dark green veggies like kale, broccoli, spinach, and bok choy.

2. A few times a week, go for orange veggies like carrots, sweet potatoes, and red or orange peppers.

3. You can look for fruits and veggies that are fresh, frozen, or even in cans.

Proteins will build and repair your muscles and bones. These include eggs, fish, dairy, beans, lentils, chicken, pork, beef, tofu, nuts, and seeds. Plant-based proteins contain more fiber and nutrients.

Try to choose whole grain foods and make water your go-to drink. Remember that healthy eating is not only about the food in front of you. Think about what you are eating and why.

Enjoy eating your meals and eat with your family whenever you can. And don't be afraid to try new things.

Eating consistent meals and snacks throughout the day will keep your energy level high. Some snacks to think about are fruit and nuts, trail mix, granola bars, and maybe even a hard-boiled egg! I know that might not sound like a type of snack, but give it a try.

Now that you know a little more about what to eat, you also need to know when to eat. Three to four hours before a training session or game, you should be eating carbohydrates, protein, and some fat along with water or a sports drink. An example would be some oatmeal (carbs) with Greek yogurt (fat) or a whole wheat chicken sandwich (protein and carbs) with some water.

One to two hours before training or a game, you will need smaller amounts of carbohydrates and protein. These portions need to be low in fat or fiber. You also need more water. An example could be a banana or a bowl of cereal with milk, washed down with water.

Thirty minutes to an hour before training or a game, you should have only a small amount of carbohydrates, and no protein or fats. This could be a piece of fruit or a small yogurt and again, some more water.

When you are traveling you will really need the help of your Integrated Support Team. Pack plenty of snacks and make sure you choose foods that your body is used to. The last thing you need is an upset stomach before the game.

Learning about what and when to eat will help you become the best soccer player you can be. And it will help you stay healthy and active long after you've finished playing soccer!

Time Management

Time management means figuring out all the things you need to do in a day and then organizing your time to make sure you do what you need to in the time you have available. As you know, we can't add time to our day. But we can build a daily schedule to help us feel like we can do what we need to do.

Each day has 24 hours, and each week has 7 days. That gives us 168 hours in one week. That might sound like a lot of time, but now we have to start thinking about all the things we have to do. There are many things that you do each day, including sleeping, eating, school, homework, meeting friends, and practicing your soccer skills. Some things, like soccer games, visiting family, or going to a friend's house, may happen on only a few days. And other things like birthday parties or sleepovers may happen occasionally.

Start by making a list of all the things you do in a week and how many hours each one takes. Start the week on Monday and work through the day. Then do Tuesday through Sunday the same way. Here is an example of what Monday could look like.

CONTINUED ON NEXT PAGE >>

Monday:

- **Sleep:** 8 hours, wake up at 6:00 a.m.
- **Get ready for school, including breakfast:** 1 hour to 7:00 a.m.
- **Travel to school:** 1 hour to 8:00 a.m.
- **School, including lunch:** 7 hours to 3:00 p.m.
- **Travel home and do homework, including a snack:** 1.5 hours, to 4:30 p.m.
- **Travel to practice:** 30 minutes to 5:00 p.m.
- **Practice:** 1.5 hours to 6:30 p.m.
- **Travel home:** 30 minutes to 7:00 p.m.
- **Time at home, including dinner, homework:** 1.5 hours to 8:30 p.m.
- **Preparing to sleep, including getting prepped for Tuesday:** 1 hour to 9:30 p.m.

You can make this as detailed or as simple as you like. The goal is to show you how your time is being used and where you can manage it better. You can ask your IST to help you start planning. Remember, there are only 24 hours each day, no more and no less. But if you make a plan and try to stick to it you will feel like you have found a little more time each day!

Your Personal Playing Pathway

When we watch the World Cup, the **Union of European Football Associations (UEFA)** Champions League, and the Olympics, we see the best athletes in the world competing at the highest level. But remember, the players that we watch don't appear in their very first game as fully finished soccer players. All of those players will have gone through the stage you are in now. That is the path that everyone takes.

In all sports, including soccer, there are athlete pathways. This is where coaches look at your age and the stage of development you are in based on how long you've played soccer, and what levels of play are available to you. The idea of a pathway is to try and support you through the different age groups all the way up into both pro and amateur adult soccer.

Here is a simple player pathway to follow. It's split into three stages, based on age.

STAGE A (8 TO 12 YEARS OLD)

At this stage, you should be playing soccer as well as other sports and activities with your friends. In soccer, you should be learning and practicing movements like speeding up, slowing down, cutting to the left and right, and stopping sharply. You should also be working on your balance, running and jumping, and learning how to land properly, then keep running. Try to play as many positions as you can so that you get to see what happens in different parts of the field and what your job is in those different areas. You'll want to get lots of touches on the ball, be juggling as often as you can, and learning and mastering as many moves as possible.

STAGE B (12 TO 16 YEARS OLD)

In this stage, you may be playing fewer sports and doing fewer activities. This is called specialization. You should now be focused on two or three positions on the soccer field so that you have some options as you move through the next stages. You don't want to be known as a player who can only play in one position. Your physical abilities will need to become stronger, and you will become fitter. You'll be spending some time in the gym working on this. You should still be practicing all of your technical skills, and you should also now be starting to understand the tactical side of the game as you make the move to the full field. You should focus on your weaker foot and make that as strong as possible. That will help you stand out from the crowd.

STAGE C (16 TO 20 YEARS OLD)

Now you will be preparing for adult soccer and that means playing with and against players who are older than you. You should be really strong in one position. Make sure you understand the different formations that different coaches use and all the strategies that are available to them. Soccer is now becoming a little more about winning, and, if they haven't already, coaches will select their team in an attempt to win games.

The biggest thing for you to remember as you start to think about your own pathway is that pathways are fluid like a river and not a straight line like a freeway. You will progress at your own pace. Sometimes it might feel like you are not moving, but the key is to keep working and you'll move forward.

Conditioning

As a young athlete you don't need a fully built out conditioning plan that includes spending time in the gym. At your age and stage of development, you really shouldn't be doing anything that includes lifting weights.

Your focus should be on developing a healthy lifestyle and making sure that you keep active each day. On days when you're not playing or training, make sure you still get at least an hour of moderate activity. Something as simple as walking to and from school if that's possible would be great.

Activities that get your heart rate up, like walking, biking, or swimming, will really help you develop a healthy lifestyle, which will benefit to you long after you have finished playing soccer.

Playing and being involved in other sports is another great way to stay healthy. You will make new friends and teammates, and the benefits of playing what we call multi-sports are huge. Almost all professional athletes were involved in a number of sports at your age. You can learn things from other sports that will help you in soccer. For example, basketball is a great way to learn how to deal with man-to-man marking and time your movements to receive the ball in space. It also helps you understand how to play zone defense and improve your body's movement patterns.

The key is to stay active.

Sleep and Rest

Every night we go to sleep, and we wake up in the morning. We really don't think about sleep and how it works, but it's an important part of being an athlete. Sleep allows our body and brain to rest. It conserves energy and helps us restock our cells so that they can prepare us for the next day. Sleep plays an important role in repairing our bodies after a tough practice or game, and in repairing injuries. It also helps our brain organize the information we are picking up all day long in the many activities we do.

Sleep works in four different stages. In the first stage, we fall into a light sleep where our body is relaxing in preparation for deeper rest. In stage two, our breathing and heart rate start to slow down. We become more relaxed and our core body temperature drops. In this stage our brain has short bursts of activity. As we move into stage three, our body begins to repair itself and our immune system is strengthened. As we move into stage four, which is called REM (rapid eye movement) sleep, we are now dreaming. Our limbs become temporarily paralyzed and the activity in our brain is now faster.

When we have a good night's sleep, ideally seven to nine uninterrupted hours, our performance is improved and our decision-making is much better. With good sleep we become better at dealing with injuries and setbacks, and we are better at dealing with stress. When we don't get enough sleep, our body craves sugar, which can disrupt our energy levels. We find it harder to concentrate and stay focused. At the same time, our reflexes slow down, and our coordination suffers. Good sleep can really help you as both a soccer player and as a student.

Here are a few tips to give yourself a better chance of good sleep:

- Set a bedtime and wake-up time that allow you to get between eight and ten hours of sleep a day.
- An hour to ninety minutes before bed, dim the lights to signal to your brain this it's time to start preparing for sleep.
- Sixty minutes before bed, turn off any of your devices and try to start slowing your brain down. This could be done by reading or stretching.
- Thirty minutes before bed, make sure your room is a dark, cool, and quiet space. The best temperature for sleep is 65 to 68°F. Also make sure your bed is clear of any clutter.

If you find that you have trouble going to sleep, be sure that you're not doing these things right before bed:

- Having a snack
- Picking up a device

Try to practice slowing your breathing down and relaxing. This can help put you in sleep mode. Focus on a simple task like counting numbers or reciting the alphabet to occupy your mind and stop it from racing around. You can also try to read a book for a few minutes; that can sometimes help you relax and put you back into sleep mode.

Ensure you go to bed at the same time each night and keep up with your sleeping routine. And remember that this is another thing that you share with your IST, so ask for help if you need it!

Pregame Routines

Another part of your success on the field comes from preparing before your game or training session. Your pregame routine starts the day *before* your game or practice. Make sure you get enough sleep. See Sleep and Rest (page 10). This means that you have this built into your plan. See Time Management (page 5).

You also need to make sure your soccer bag is packed. Make sure your kit is fresh and clean, and that you have all the things you need in your bag for the game along with some extras. It's important for you to prepare your own bag so you know you have what you need. You can ask your IST for help, but you should take responsibility for your preparation.

As you pack your bag, make sure you have enough snacks to get you through the day and enough water to keep you hydrated. See Eating to Succeed (page 3).

Work with your IST to figure out how to get to the field on time. If you're late, you'll be the one who risks playing time. If there is ever a time that you know you will be late, make sure that you let the coach know. Coaches have their own pregame routines to follow, so it's helpful to know if someone is going to be late or can't make it.

Before the start of the game or training, your coach may have a set warm-up for you to do. It's important to follow their direction, but if you know that you need a longer warm-up, then you have to make a little more time for yourself.

PART 2

Techniques

You practice technique, but you display skill. A technique is something you do in isolation. It isn't connected to any other event or movement. In this section of the book, we are going to look at individual skills that you have total control over. This means you can improve your ability to perform them by doing one thing: practicing! Many of these techniques are fairly simple to practice on your own, without an opponent. Eventually, the learned technique will become a skill. These impressive improved skills will up your game on the field and your status as a team player.

Performing a technique when you are practicing alone is one thing, but you have to be able to do the technique in-game. We call this *performance on demand*, and believe me, it's important! The ability to perform on demand and in the heat of competition comes not just from skill, but from having confidence in your ability to complete simple techniques in not-so-simple situations. It's highly unlikely that you will be successful the very first time you try a new skill. You may get lucky, but the reality is that we learn by failing. The more you practice, the closer you will get to mastering the skills of soccer.

In sports, there are many things outside of your control. The good news is that your level of technical expertise is totally up to you. You got this book because you want to get better. Remember this mantra: try, fail, try again—fail better!

LEVEL ❶ ② ③

Setting Goals

TYPE OF TECHNIQUE: Personal development

This technique is about your ambitions and dreams for playing soccer—not the kind of goals when the ball blasts past the keeper. Without a plan for these kinds of achievable personal goals, you are simply going along from one game to the next with no way of assessing how you did. How can you grow if all you remember is whether it was a good game or bad game?

So, what do we mean when we talk about setting achievable goals? We can pick out all kinds of goals, but are they realistic? I remember wanting to be an astronaut and go to Mars. Sure, that's a goal, but there were a few things standing in my way. (140 million miles, to be a little more precise. Oh, and no breathable air!)

There are outcome (results) goals, such as getting to Mars, being MVP, being the top scorer, or winning the state championship. There are process (action) goals, such as increasing your level of fitness, getting into good positions in the opponent's penalty area, or receiving fewer yellow cards for arguing on the field. The difference between these two types of goals is vital.

With *outcome* goals, you are not fully in control of the situation. You have no way of being sure you can achieve that goal. Going to Mars is a lot different from being the top scorer, but the theory is the same. Other people are scoring goals and goalkeepers are trying to stop you from scoring. You can have the best season of your life, but someone else might have a better one. If you look at *process* goals, you are in total control of the situation or action. To increase your level of fitness, you figure out how to work out better and smarter. To not get yellow cards for arguing on the field, well, stop arguing on the field. *You* have the power to achieve a process goal. These are better goals to set for yourself.

TRY IT

First, think about the goals you'd like to set. Maybe your first thought is: *I want to have a good season.* How can you measure your performance to see whether you are achieving this goal? At the risk of sounding obvious, if you want to measure something, it has to be measurable. What is your definition of good, and how will you assess your performance? Is it goal scoring? Completed passes? Improved technique? Where do you stand now, and where do you want to go? The best way to assess yourself is to get someone to record you in a game or two so that you can watch your current level of performance. You can only know if you've improved later if you know where you are today.

Here are some ideas for achievable goals in fitness and performance:

- Look at agility tests. Set them up with a partner and a stopwatch. See how you improve over a month, season, or year.
- Measure the number of completed passes you make during games and practice, and convert it to a percentage. How much better would you like to get? Be realistic. If your starting percentage is 20 percent, a goal of 100 percent in the season is a bit too aggressive. What percentage does the best player on the team have? Aim for something a little lower than that for now.
- How often do you regain possession? Look at numbers over the course of a few games. What is the average? You can control and improve this number by being an active defender.

All of these goal examples are measurable. There are plenty of other goals you can set for yourself. Make sure you have control over them. I bet a friend, coach, or other active adult would help track your goals. Keep at it!

You can also set some longer-term goals for your soccer career. See Your Personal Playing Pathway (page 7). One of your goals could be to make the high school team and start as a junior. Or you might challenge yourself to make the varsity squad as a freshman in college. Maybe you want to get some minutes as a freshman, start a game as a sophomore, and be a starter as a junior. Setting longer-term goals will mean a lot of work, but if you want to keep playing, keep giving yourself goals to achieve. This gives you a focus that your peers might not have, and that's a great advantage!

COACH'S CORNER TIPS

No matter what level you play at—no matter what sport or activity you play—*you* are in charge of becoming the best player you can be! Set goals, ask for help, and be flexible when your personal plan changes.

Developing Your Philosophy

LEVEL **1** 2 3

TYPE OF TECHNIQUE: Staying sharp

You might think that developing a philosophy, whether that is a soccer philosophy or a life philosophy, isn't a technique that you need in soccer. But it's a key part of becoming and staying an effective athlete. Having a personal philosophy will help you make decisions not only on the field, but also in life. Whether you realize it or not, the way you view the world affects your play. Your personal philosophy decides what you think is right or wrong, what acceptable behavior is, what you expect from your teammates, and what they should expect from you. For example, we all want to get an edge when we play, but how far will you go to get that edge? Is cheating okay as long as you can get away with it? Personally, I don't think so. If we have to cheat to win, then we didn't really win. Winning can become more important, and it may for you as you get older. But for now, enjoying the games and training sessions, being active, and meeting new friends should be part of your philosophy.

Here is a philosophy that might help you come up with your own. It's from the legendary New England Patriots coach, Bill Belichick. He simply told his players, "Do your job." A really simple but great message.

When building your philosophy, you must decide what you believe and what you stand for. It's not *thinking* what you believe, but *living* what you believe. To put it another way: You are what you do. Don't say that fair play and respect are important to you if all you do is argue with the officials during every game. Bailing on your philosophy tells you something about what type of person you are. It shows what you want Future You to look like. You are the only one who can change it.

TRY IT

This exercise will take a different set of muscles—your brain and your writing/typing hands. Write a paragraph about what you believe in and how you want to be perceived by teammates and opponents. It might include believing in fair play, being a supportive teammate, being a humble winner but also a good loser, working hard, acting ethically, or any number of things that you believe to be important.

Now take that paragraph and try to cut it down to no more than thirty-two words. You're trying to prioritize and narrow it down in a way that is easy to remember. A version of it will become your mantra to help you focus before a game and refocus during the game.

Now take it down to sixteen words. Keep only the concepts or phrases most important to you.

From here I challenge you to go to no more than eight words (yes, eight!). These are the eight words that will become your mantra. They can be a list of what you value, such as "honesty, sportsmanship, skills, loyalty to teammates, daily practice." Or they can make up a short sentence, such as "Put in my best effort regardless of others." There is no right or wrong here. Play around with it for a while. You can always come back and change it. They are your words, no one else's. Honor them and keep them close.

COACH'S CORNER TIPS

We learn best when we learn from other people. Look for role models in your life or sport and think about how they can help you achieve your own goals.

Look Up!

LEVEL ① ❷ ③

TYPE OF TECHNIQUE: Attacking, ball manipulation; defending, 1v1 and zonal

ATTACKING PLAYER TO WATCH: Luka Modrić, player for Tottenham Hotspur, Real Madrid, AC Milan, and Croatia

GAME TO WATCH: 2018 World Cup semifinal, Croatia vs. England

DEFENDING PLAYER TO WATCH: Virgil van Dijk, player for Groningen, Celtic, Southampton, Liverpool and the Netherlands

GAME TO WATCH: 2019 Champions League final, Liverpool vs. Tottenham Hotspur

---

The expression "get your head in the game" means staying focused. In soccer, going from good to great means having great technique and outstanding decision-making abilities. In order to make good decisions, you need as much information as possible. You can't make good decisions without enough information, and you can't get enough information if you aren't paying attention. If you have your head up, you can see what is happening around you, figure out the best path to take, and make the best decisions on what to do next. If you don't have the ball, you need to keep your head up to be able to predict where the ball will go next and get in position. To get your head in the game, you have to look up!

TRY IT

When you were just learning to play, you looked down a lot. It's not that you didn't know whether the ball was there; it's that you weren't sure exactly where it was. As a result, you got used to looking down even though you didn't always need to, and it became a habit. A good exercise to break this habit is to take a ball at your feet and look ahead. Without looking down at the ball, roll it forward until you can just see it appearing in the bottom of your visual range. This gives you an idea of what your natural blind spot is. It also lets you know when you can see the ball naturally when looking ahead.

In a 15-by-15 yard area (as if you were turning the penalty box area into a full square instead of a rectangle), take the ball and go through your normal warm-up and dribbling patterns. Your goal is to limit your glances to the ground while staying in control of the ball (and not stepping on it!). Try to take a quick look down on every third touch. I think you will master this technique pretty quickly. The key here is to have small touches, like you are just prodding the ball.

Got that down pat? Now try to glance down on every fourth touch. Then try to glance every fifth touch, but remember to keep the ball close. Once you feel you have mastered this technique, set up some cones to dribble through or around while looking up. Be prepared to make some errors, and maybe even fall over the ball a few times. It happens. Doing that in practice is a lot better than doing it in a game. See Ball Manipulation (page 164) for how to practice this drill.

On the defensive side of the ball, you also need to get your head up in order to recognize the situation in front of you and what you need to do. See Zonal Marking (page 86), Man-to-Man Marking (page 89), Defending from the Front Line (page 92), Defending Against Their Playmaker (page 94), and Pressing to Get the Ball Back (page 96).

COACH'S CORNER TIPS

When something in a game or training session doesn't go the way you thought it would, embrace the challenge. It's an opportunity to learn something new.

1v1 Against the Keeper

TYPE OF TECHNIQUE: Attacking, ball control, shooting, dribbling

PLAYER TO WATCH: Fernando Torres, player for Atlético Madrid, Liverpool, Chelsea, AC Milan, and Spain

GAME TO WATCH: 2012 Champions League semifinal, Chelsea vs. Barcelona

At this stage in your soccer career, you know a little about shooting against the keeper. But in this section we will go into more detail.

Imagine you are almost at the goal. You have beaten the offside trap with a well-timed run, and you are in the clear with just the keeper to beat. Now what? As you move forward, the things to focus on are the ball, the keeper, and the goal line—in that order. If you lose control of the ball for a second, you give the advantage to the keeper. You need to be aware of the keeper's movements so you can time your decision on when and where to shoot.

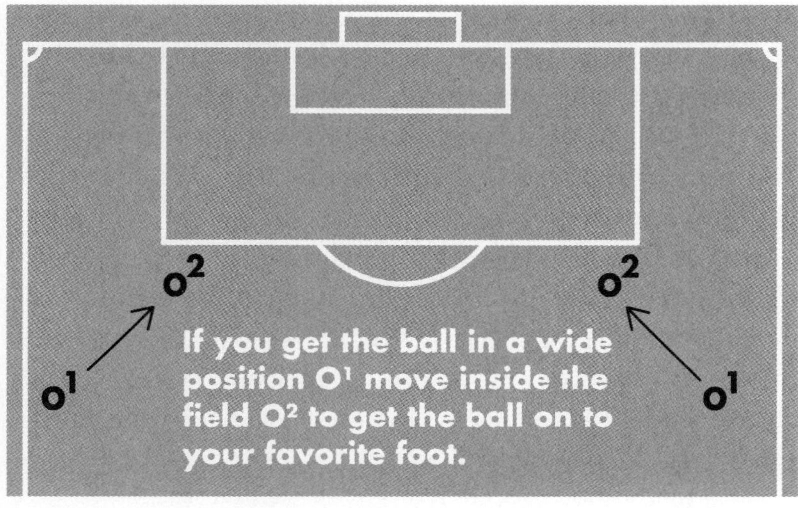

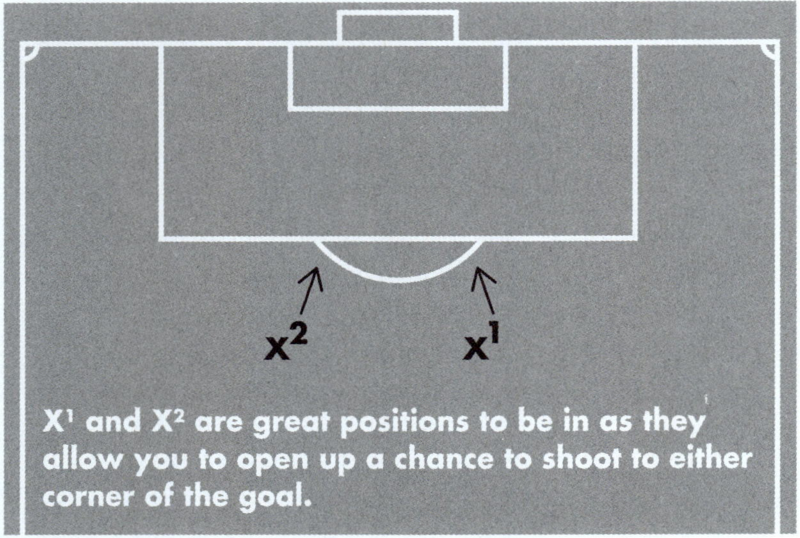

X^1 and X^2 are great positions to be in as they allow you to open up a chance to shoot to either corner of the goal.

TRY IT

The first thing I suggest in a 1v1 against the goalkeeper when running in a straight line down the center of the field is to take a touch with the ball to your strong side (left-footed player to the left, right-footed player to the right). See positions X^1 and X^2 on the diagram above. This will open up some angles for you and give you the option of bending the ball around the goalkeeper to the **near post** or striking the ball across the goalkeeper's body into the **far post**. When you have this touch, make sure that your head is up so you can see the goalkeeper. You need to be aware of their position! Use the inside of your foot with the toe slightly raised. This is much easier when you are approaching the goal **on an angle**.

If you see the keeper come off their line, go for the chip over their head into the open goal. This is a great option when you are on an angle to the center of the goal, and not lined up down the center line. See Chipping the Ball (page 46) for how to practice this technique.

If the keeper is staying closer to the line, be sure to keep your head up. Why? When we train keepers, we tell them to look for the oncoming player's head going down as the signal they are setting up for a shot. By keeping your head up, you'll give them one less clue about what you're going to do.

If you are going for the near post, as you approach the keeper, strike the ball on the outside so that it spins counterclockwise, with your toe slightly raised to increase the spin. Focus on doing this in stride so that the keeper doesn't see it coming. If you are going for the far post, then your last touch before you shoot needs to be a small touch to your strong side, to allow you to open up your hips to get more power. On contact, your toe should be pointed down with the heel above the toe, to keep the ball down. In this instance you are going for accuracy. Think about this as a controlled pass into the net.

COACH'S CORNER TIPS

Good athletes are never on time; they are early. Do your best to arrive at practice or games early to warm up and be fully prepared. Failing to prepare is preparing to fail!

LEVEL

Free Kicks

TYPE OF TECHNIQUE: Attacking, ball striking

PLAYER TO WATCH: David Beckham, player for Manchester United, Real Madrid, AC Milan, Paris Saint-Germain, LA Galaxy, and England

GAME TO WATCH: 2001 World Cup Qualifier, England vs. Greece

PLAYER TO WATCH: Declan Rice, player for West Ham United, Arsenal, and England

GAME TO WATCH: 2025 Champions League quarterfinal, Arsenal vs. Real Madrid

There are two types of free kicks: the direct free kick and the indirect free kick. It's important, regardless of what type of free kick you are taking, that your team is on the same page. Make sure everyone knows what the play is going to be, who the pass is going to, and what that person will do with the ball once they get it. There is nothing more frustrating for a team than to see an intricate free kick routine go wrong. It means time on the training field has been wasted, and every opportunity in the game hasn't been taken.

TRY IT

Any free kick that isn't within shooting range of the opponent's goal should be thought of as an indirect kick, because you won't be scoring directly from that position. The best technique for each free kick will depend on where it is on the field and what is going on at the time. In my opinion, when it comes to free kicks awarded to your team in your **defending third**, get on the ball quickly and play it forward to an open player. It keeps the game moving, and while the opposition are arguing about the foul, you are moving forward. Your focus here is on being able to make a good pass to an unmarked player, using good technique. That means the non-kicking foot is placed facing the target, the ankle is locked on contact, and there is good follow-through. If you can't see a simple pass, though, take your time with this one.

In the **middle third**, a quick free kick becomes a stronger option because it might get you into the attacking zone. If you can get to the ball quickly and go forward, or you see an opportunity to switch play to an open teammate, take that option. Free kicks are valuable, but more goals come from open play. The focus here is on pass selection and making sure that the player receiving the ball is aware that it's coming. Communication becomes almost as important as your technique and pass selection.

When you are in the **attacking third**, things change. If you are awarded an indirect kick where it's close enough for the second touch to score, it's important for everyone to know the plan. If the first touch of the ball is setting up a shot, remember that the ball has to be seen to be moving. It can't just be a tap on the ball. Timing and coordination are really important. Focus on the ball whether you are taking the touch or taking the shot.

If it's a direct kick and you are shooting on goal, set the ball in the spot you want it and make sure you get the best approach to the ball. Regardless of the technique you choose, make sure that you do two things: First, get the ball either around the wall or over the wall of players; hitting the wall is not an option. Second, and perhaps more ideally, make the keeper move. If you can fake out the keeper and they zip over in the wrong direction, then it's a goal. Power is nothing without control. See Free Kicks (page 161) for how to practice this drill.

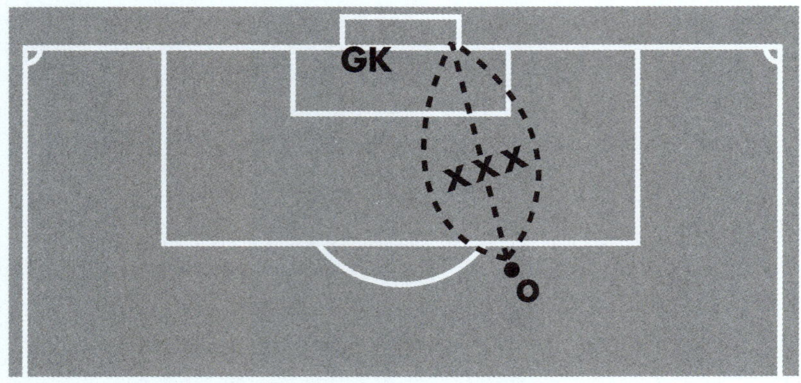

In the diagram above, the player can go to either side of the wall or over the middle of the wall from where the ball is placed. If you choose to go to the left side of the wall, from this space, you can use the position of the ball to shoot to the far corner of the goal or try to bend the ball into the near post. Shooting over the middle of the wall gives you less of an angle to use. And as players get taller, going over the middle of the wall becomes more challenging, as you have to control the ball to get it up over the wall and down under the crossbar. See Chipping the Ball (page 46) for this type of free kick. If you choose to go to the right side of the wall, you can use the ball position to go the far corner of the goal or try for the near post.

COACH'S CORNER TIPS

Self-talk is using that little voice we all have in our heads to encourage and motivate us. You can use self-talk on the field, at school, or even at home to help you build self-confidence.

Penalties

TYPE OF TECHNIQUE: Attacking, shooting, ball striking

PLAYER TO WATCH: Harry Kane, player for Tottenham Hotspur, Bayern Munich, and England

GAME TO WATCH: 2024 Euro semifinal, England vs. Netherlands

PLAYER TO WATCH: Chloe Kelly, player for Everton, Arsenal, Manchester City, and England

GAME TO WATCH: 2023 Women's Finalissima, England vs. Brazil

There are two different options for penalties, and I'll go into both here. Taking penalties is simply about ball-striking technique and hitting a target from twelve yards out. The challenge is that the one person trying to **block** the ball can use their hands. If you think I am simplifying things a little, then you are correct.

Taking penalties is part technique and part mental focus. If you have good technique in terms of ball striking, then you will increase your chances of scoring from pretty much any spot. Everyone misses penalties, and goalkeepers make some great stops, but if you always hit the target then you are making the keeper stop it. You want to avoid missing the target.

Let's start with some basic math. A professional goal is 24 feet long and 8 feet high, totaling 192 square feet of space. Let's say that at full stretch, the keeper's body and arms cover 15 square feet. That leaves around 177 square feet of space to put the ball in. (Sounds easy that way, doesn't it?) The key, of course, is to put the ball where the keeper *isn't*. There are two different ways of doing this: You can pick your favorite spot and slap it there like clockwork, or you can wait and watch to see where the keeper goes to shoot it into a different spot. The key to both is your confidence in your own technique.

TRY IT

If you are aiming for a spot, you need Plan A, which is most likely your strongest foot into the opposite corner. (If you are right-footed then you kick to your left, and if you are left-footed you kick to your right.) Plan B is your option if you have taken penalty kicks against the keeper before and think you can predict their moves, or you want to wait for them to dive one way and shoot the other way. The choice of Plan A or B is mental; everything after that is technique.

In terms of any technique, I suggest aiming low to the ground, as no one ever put the ball under the goal! Regardless of where you are shooting, decide where the ball is going before you start your run-up. Know where it will land. Visualize it. At the very start, look down to focus on the ball and the planting of your non-kicking foot. This should be about one and a half to two of your own feet's width from the ball, with your ankle planted just ahead of the center of the ball to generate power. Lock your ankle on contact and strike through the ball, toe down, keeping your toe below your ankle on the follow-through. You can practice this technique on your own, over and over and over again. Pick the same spot every time, or choose a different spot every time to see if you end up having a favorite. Once you've got the mental confidence, bring in a goalkeeper to shoot against.

If you are going to try to send the keeper the wrong way, approach the ball with your head up so that you are looking directly at them. This also prevents them from predicting your move. You will most likely use a side-foot kick, so your non-kicking foot will be planted one to one and a half of your own foot's width away from the ball. You are going for a good strike with less power but more finesse. As you approach the ball from a shorter run-up, keep your eye on the keeper. If they move, shoot to the opposite side. If they come forward, send it low to the corner. Of course, if they leave the line early, it should be a retake. Practicing against a real keeper is the only way to help you make decisions on the fly.

Trying to send the keeper the wrong way is quite a bit harder than just going for it into your favorite spot. It takes a little more confidence, because you are waiting for the keeper to move. As with everything else in soccer, you won't master this straightaway. However, if you choose this method and you are successful, you will become a real asset to your team. Have you seen how many playoff, cup games, and finals are decided on penalties?

COACH'S CORNER TIPS

Learn how to accept short, clear instructions from your coach in a game or training session. It's important to make sure you know what your coach wants from you. In the game there isn't always time for a long explanation.

MEET THE SOCCER STAR
AITANA BONMATÍ

Birth Date: January 18, 1998

Position: Midfielder

Teams: Barcelona and Spain

Aitana Bonmatí was born in Sant Pere de Ribes in Catalonia, Spain. She is one of the brightest stars in the world of women's soccer. She started playing soccer at seven years old for her local boys' team, CD Ribes. The club had 400 players, but she was the only girl! After four years, Aitana moved on to a new club, Cubelles, and in 2012 she moved to Barcelona, where she's helped the team dominate women's soccer in Spain and Europe. She's won multiple trophies with her club team, as well as with the National Women's team of Spain, and many individual honors.

Aitana grew up in a small town and spent the first few years of her life learning resilience, focus, and concentration. Her parents encouraged her to piece together puzzles. These skills helped her develop into a soccer star with a strong character, and fit in and be accepted as a teammate.

When she joined Barcelona, she had to take a bus and a train to practice each day. It was a tiring commute, which was hard on her, and she considered quitting. Aitana's mother suggested that she talk to a sport psychologist, who helped her realize her frustrations were part of her pursuit of excellence. It wasn't an easy journey for Aitana, but she managed to stay in the program.

Although she is now recognized as one of the best in the world, she didn't start with this success. At the age of twenty-one she was not a starter and was on the outside of the team. But her strong character and puzzle-solving ability helped her break into the team, and the rest is history.

LEVEL ① ② ❸

Long-Range Shooting

TYPE OF TECHNIQUE: Attacking, ball striking

PLAYER TO WATCH: Steven Gerrard, player for Liverpool, LA Galaxy, and England

GAME TO WATCH: 2006 FA Cup Final, Liverpool vs. West Ham United

The ability to hit a target from a long distance will distinguish you from other players in your age group. When you shoot from a distance, the focus must be on clean contact with the ball in order to generate power. You are not really trying to pick out a spot in the goal where you think you can beat the keeper. Instead, you are looking to cause maximum stress on the goal-keeper by striking the ball as cleanly and powerfully as you can and then leaving the rest to the ball.

When shooting from a distance, there are basically two types of setups. The first is when you are in control of the ball and you have the last touch to set the ball up before the strike. The second is when the ball is rolling toward you after a touch from another player. The more you can control the ball, the more you can generate power and therefore have a greater chance of scoring.

TRY IT

Start by looking at the landing spot when you set the ball up. The touch before your shot should be to the side of your stronger foot. By pushing the ball to the side, you create a space that allows you to open up your hips and have a greater backswing onto the ball. This lets you generate more force. Push the ball out to the side, positioning your **plant foot** with your toes slightly **ahead of the ball** by about three to four times the width of your foot, in order to give your kicking foot enough room to come through. Keep your eyes on the ball (you know where the goal is). Bring your foot through the ball with your ankle locked, toes down, and heel up, and kick using your instep. As you strike the ball, try to get your plant foot off the ground, so all your force is transferred through the kicking foot to the ball.

If the ball is coming at you instead of sitting stationary in the field, it allows you to generate more power. But you still need to control the ball. As the ball comes toward you, get your eyes on it as soon as possible and try to figure out where you will strike it. Approach the strike zone, get your plant foot set, and bring your kicking foot through the ball. On contact it's vital that you are leaning slightly forward, because this will help you keep the ball down. Your kicking foot should be ankle-locked with toes down. Contact comes from the instep with a smooth follow-through. In this instance, keep your plant foot on the ground, so that on contact you are grounded and as balanced as possible. It will help you have more control over the ball. See Long-Range Shooting (page 162) for how to practice this drill.

COACH'S CORNER TIPS

Athletes become mentally tough by recognizing what is important to focus on. Manage what you can manage; the rest is all noise you can ignore.

Shooting Inside the Penalty Area, Inside the 18

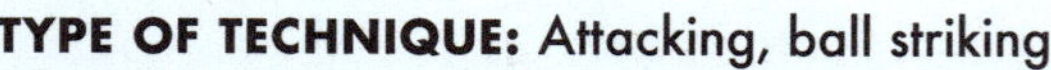

TYPE OF TECHNIQUE: Attacking, ball striking

PLAYER TO WATCH: Neymar, player for Santos, Al Hilal, Paris Saint-Germain, Barcelona, and Brazil

GAME TO WATCH: 2016 Barcelona vs. Villareal

The penalty area, also known as **the 18** or "the box," is nerve-racking. In a crowded penalty area, a lot of things can happen to help you, so it's not all bad. Shots can be deflected into the goal, the ball can hit a defender's hand, or you can be awarded a penalty. Playing close to one another increases the chances of a foul, which could also lead to a penalty. When you find yourself in this position, the last thing you want is a wild swing at the ball and a shot that flies high and wide!

The first thing you need to do is define what is a good shot in this situation: It's a strike toward the goal, preferably below shoulder height, made from a player who is set and balanced on contact. In order to make a good shot, it's important to make the decision to shoot as early as possible.

Believing in your ability to perform good technique in your shot is equally important. Confidence in your technique is half the battle.

TRY IT

You have some decisions to make. Which part of the foot are you going to strike the ball with—the side of your foot or your instep? The side foot will give you greater accuracy, as there is more surface area; your instep will give you a little more power and force. Where are you aiming—the near post, far post, or a

specific point through the goal line? Remember, lower is almost always better. Visualize it. Now get your eye on the ball and your feet set.

With your feet in place and your eyes focused firmly on the ball, strike through the ball, leaning forward on contact. Striking the ball on the equator helps keep the ball low. If the ball rises too high, not only is it easier for the goalkeeper to catch, but it also might go over the bar. If shooting with your instep, make sure your toes don't come above your heel in the follow-through.

In the 18, you should always be thinking about what is going to happen next. The play may not be over as soon as you kick it. Get your head up immediately after contact and be prepared, because there is a good chance the shot may be deflected back toward you or to another team member. You need to be ready for what comes next. You won't score every time, but you won't miss every time. And if you don't take the shot, then you most certainly won't score a goal!

COACH'S CORNER TIPS

You decide how you show up to a game or training session, no one else. Own your commitment and attitude.

LEVEL ① ❷ ③

Running with the Ball

TYPE OF TECHNIQUE: Attacking, ball movement

PLAYER TO WATCH: Theo Walcott, player for Southampton, Arsenal, and Everton

GAME TO WATCH: 2008 Champions League quarterfinal, Arsenal vs. Liverpool

The quickest way to move the ball in soccer is by passing. The ball never gets tired, and it travels faster than the player. However, since you are still in possession in open runs, you can also take advantage of the disruptions you create to help move members of the defending team. As players move toward you, they leave an open space. At times they will leave a teammate open. If you can take advantage of this disruption, you will play a part in creating scoring chances.

In order to be successful at running with the ball, you need to decide when it's the right time. It's important that you play with your head up and are aware of the spaces around you. I suggest you keep at least fifteen to twenty yards of free space when running toward the opponent's goal. The key to this skill is your stride pattern and ability to push the ball forward without breaking the pattern. Fewer touches allow for more speed. Your job is to find the balance between running speed and keeping possession. If your touch is too heavy, you will most likely lose the ball.

TRY IT

When running with the ball, make sure that it is always in front of you upon contact. To do this, contact the ball with your little toe. Your foot should be pointing down with the heel up as you push the ball forward with the outside of your foot. Using this technique allows you to push the ball forward in your normal stride, which means that you don't have to break your stride or slow down.

Stride pattern is important. As you start your run, make sure that you have the ball under control. The pattern is touch-step-touch. Broken down, that means you touch the ball with your outer foot, step and land on your non-kicking foot, and then complete another touch that's more like a nudge with your kicking foot. These touches are about five yards apart, which allows you to start building your speed while keeping control of the ball. A heavy touch here may lead to you losing possession.

Once you've gained speed, if you've beaten your opponent, you will have more space to continue to commit to the run. From here, you will change your stride pattern. Your next touches need to be farther away, since the ball will be farther away from you as you run faster. It will now be touch-step-step-step-step-touch. Do it this way: Touch with your kicking foot and land, step forward on your non-kicking foot, stride and land with your kicking foot, then land one more time with your non-kicking foot before pushing the ball again with the outside of your kicking foot. You have now increased the distance between touches and decreased the number of touches. See Running with the Ball (page 163) for how to practice this drill.

COACH'S CORNER TIPS

Learn to be comfortable being uncomfortable. Not everything will go your way in a game or training session. Figure out how to deal with it and keep moving forward.

LEVEL ① ❷ ③

Speed Dribbling

TYPE OF TECHNIQUE: Attacking, ball manipulation

PLAYER TO WATCH: Raheem Sterling, player for Liverpool, Manchester City, Chelsea, and England

GAME TO WATCH: 2023 Chelsea vs. Luton Town

First off, speed dribbling is not the same as running with the ball. Both involve speed and ball control. What's the difference, then? When running with the ball, you're knocking the ball from your feet into space as you run, and catching up with the ball as you go. With speed dribbling, you're running with the ball much closer in, keeping it guarded.

To cover a long distance, a pass is more effective. Running with the ball covers more ground as well. Why do you dribble the ball in soccer at all then, if it's the least effective way of moving the ball over a long distance? There are a couple of reasons. First, dribbling lets you draw opponents to the ball. Bringing the other player toward you creates space for a teammate to make themselves available for a pass. Second, dribbling sets you up to make a move to beat any defender that is drawn toward you.

In order to be successful at speed dribbling, you need good balance, agility, and body control. The only difference between speed dribbling and regular dribbling is that you are moving much faster (as you probably figured out). Control of the ball and your body become much more important at pace.

When speed dribbling, you can use different parts of your foot as you are not primarily concerned with covering space quickly. It's more about control of the ball and drawing in opponents. Technique-wise, it's pretty much the same as running with the ball, but there are some small changes in direction, going from side to side in order to unbalance your opponent.

TRY IT

The pattern for speed dribbling is touch-step-touch-step. You don't want to push the ball any farther than five yards away in order to maintain control. At times, as defenders approach, that distance may be shorter. In order to speed dribble, use the inside of your foot to cut **inside**, and the outside of your foot to cut **outside**. Think of yourself as bait on the end of a fishing pole being pulled through the water. You are doing the same job, trying to attract attention and isolate a defender.

It is best to look at your opponent's hips when you're speed dribbling, because they will give you some clue as to when the defender is off-balance and tell you when to make your move. Once you have engaged the defender, dribble right at their feet to freeze them in position.

In order to practice speed dribbling, you will need to set up a space that's fifteen yards long with two cones. The aim is to get across that space as quickly as possible with the ball under control. If you can get someone to time your runs with a stopwatch, all the better! As you practice, your goal is to try to increase the number of touches you have on the ball inside the fifteen yards. On your first try, aim to get three touches in and stop the ball on the far cone. If you can stop the ball, it means that you are in control of the ball. Focus on increasing the number of touches to five without losing speed. If you get to five touches, try to include touches with different parts of your feet so that you can start to get small directional changes in your approach to the opponent. Soon you'll be able to dodge side to side.

COACH'S CORNER TIPS

When learning a new skill, break it down into smaller chunks at first so you master the technique. Then put it all together.

LEVEL ① ❷ ❸

Volleys and Half Volleys

TYPE OF TECHNIQUE: Attacking, shot on goal

PLAYER TO WATCH: Zinedine Zidane, player for Cannes, Bordeaux, Juventus, Real Madrid, and France

GAME TO WATCH: 2002 Champions League Final, Real Madrid vs. Bayer Leverkusen

Personally, I have always found the half volley to be a harder skill than the volley. I have to react a little later to the bounce of the ball and keep track of it onto my kicking foot. That's why I have the half volley level of difficulty as a 3. I'd suggest you work on that skill first and then move to the volley.

A full volley is when you strike the ball out of the air before it touches the ground after it has been played by another player. As you know, perfecting the volley is one of the most demanding things in the game. But when it works, it's something special.

A half volley is when you strike the ball after it has bounced. A clean half volley is also a difficult skill to learn, because there is a timing element to the half volley that isn't part of the full volley.

In all volleys, you use the pace of the ball as it is coming to you to generate power.

TRY IT

With half volleys, you strike at knee level or below. If you need to hit a half volley above your knee, I suggest you control the ball first, and then make a decision. Timing is now important. Some coaches will say that you hit the ball as it's rising, because that can help you generate power. I think you can generate power through timing, and that when striking a half volley, you should strike the ball just as it's coming back down to the ground. This will help you keep the ball down, because you will strike the ball on or slightly above the equator. If you can strike a half volley toward the ground, then you get the advantage of the bounce, which changes it in flight. That's a huge advantage against the keeper. As you approach the ball, get to the spot early and get in position. With your eye on the ball, keep your feet moving so that you make late adjustments to the bounce, and when the ball starts to drop from its bounce, follow the script for the full volley. See Half Volleys (page 164) and Juggling (page 163) for how to practice these drills.

With a full volley, get your eyes on the ball. As the ball is coming to you, get in position to strike. Plant your non-kicking foot to provide balance. On contact, you should be leaning forward slightly and a little to your left if you are striking with the right foot, and to the right if you are striking with your left foot. This gives you the space to bring your kicking foot through in a controlled manner so you aren't swinging at the ball and sending it farther than you want it to go. Make sure your toe is down and use your instep to strike through the ball with your ankle in a locked position. Don't bring your toe up on the follow-through.

COACH'S CORNER TIPS

After every practice and game, no matter whether you won or lost, had a good personal performance or not, focus on something positive. Remember it and leave the field with a smile on your face.

MEET THE SOCCER STAR
CHRISTIAN PULISIC

Birth Date: September 18, 1998

Positions: Winger, attacking midfielder

Teams: Borussia Dortmund, Chelsea, AC Milan, and the United States

Christian Pulisic was born in Hershey, Pennsylvania. He had soccer in his DNA as both of his parents played collegiate soccer at George Mason University. When his mother was teaching in England, Christian got to play for Brackley Town in Northamptonshire—his first English club!

On his return to the United States, Christian joined the PA Classics in his hometown. He also spent some time training with his local pro club, the Harrisburg City Islanders.

In early 2019, Christian returned to English football and signed with Chelsea. In his first season, he scored eleven goals and had ten assists. One of those goals was in the FA Cup Final, making him the first American player to score in the tournament's final game.

Christian moved to the Italian club AC Milan in July 2023, where has continued to develop and is a key member of the *Rossoneri*, or the Red and Blacks, as they are known. Christian is also a key member of the U.S. Men's National Team.

Christian has a very versatile attacking style of play. He can play all across the front line on either wing or in a central position. He makes runs into dangerous areas of the field and is good at stretching the opposition's back line. When he's on the ball, he is skilled at making passes to teammates. He also helps his team in defense as he is always ready to work hard to win back possession of the ball. This collection of skills alongside his direct dribbling makes Christian Pulisic the complete modern player.

LEVEL 1 2 3

Mid-Range Passing (Instep)

TYPE OF TECHNIQUE: Passing, ball striking

PLAYER TO WATCH: Luka Modrić, player for Tottenham Hotspur, Real Madrid, AC Milan, and Croatia

GAME TO WATCH: 2018 Champions League Final, Real Madrid vs. Liverpool

---

Since passing is the most effective way to get the ball from A to B, being able to deliver mid-range passes from fifteen to twenty-five yards away accurately and consistently will help you play at higher levels of the game. While many people focus on longer passes that can change a game, the mid-range pass has a greater impact throughout the full game. This pass allows you to move the ball quickly and sets up the next series of moves that can lead to goal-scoring opportunities.

We use this style of pass often when we regain possession from either an interception or tackle. Accurate mid-range passes allow us to move the ball away from where the opponent has more players than us, and make sure we keep possession. Some of the most successful teams in the world have mastered this skill and are able to stretch the opposition's back line in order to create free space for their players to run into, as well as to isolate their skillful players in 1v1 situations.

TRY IT

The focus here is on a clean strike, preferably along the ground, so that when the ball is received by your teammate, it is easy to deal with. Because you are striking the ball with your instep, there needs to be enough room for your kicking foot to come through and strike the ball. Your non-kicking foot needs to be a little farther away from the ball so you can get a good backswing to generate power in the strike. Your non-kicking foot should be somewhere around three times the width of your foot away from the ball, pointing in the direction you want the ball to go. See if you can get someone to record a few of your strikes to help you get your feet in the right place.

On contact, your toe should be down and your heel should be up with your ankle joint locked. This will help you get the power you need for a crisp pass. Make sure you are leaning slightly forward and aiming to strike through the center of the ball. All these things will help keep the ball low to the ground. After you strike the ball, make sure that you land on your kicking foot. You want to start moving to the next place you need to be in order to support the player you just passed to.

COACH'S CORNER TIPS

Shift your focus from winning or losing to the effort you put into training and the progress you make over time. If you're improving, you're winning, no matter the outcome of a game.

LEVEL 1 2 3

Chipping the Ball

TYPE OF TECHNIQUE: Passing, shooting, dead ball situations

PLAYER TO WATCH: Glenn Hoddle, player for Tottenham Hotspur, Monaco, Swindon Town, and Chelsea

GAME TO WATCH: September 1983, Tottenham Hotspur vs. Watford

What is "chipping" the ball and when do we do it? A chip is when the ball starts on the ground, gets high quickly, and drops without bouncing away. Backspin keeps the ball in place.

You chip the ball when you want the ball to go up and down in a short space. For example, you might chip the ball from a corner kick into the near post or over the back line of the opponent's defense for a striker to run onto in open play. The backspin really helps, as it stops the ball from getting away from the player running to it. You could also use the chipping technique when taking free kicks in central areas that are close to the edge of the 18-yard box, or the penalty area. When chipping the ball from a stationary position such as a corner or free kick, you are looking to get maximum lift as you have to get the ball over a person who is only ten yards away.

TRY IT

Place the ball and get your non-kicking foot in position, pointing at the target. Make contact with the ball where it touches the ground, and make sure your toe is down. Contact the ball with the knuckle of your big toe. As you go to hit the ball, your cleats should be in contact with the ground, since you are trying to scoop your foot under the ball to get it into the air quickly. Lean back just a little bit as you lift your kicking foot. It's almost like you are going to balance the ball on your toes for a second before releasing (but you're not!). Control your follow-through, because this action will increase the backspin and help the ball drop faster. The ball will ideally land either under the crossbar or on a teammate's head at the near post, where they can **flick it on**.

If you are looking for distance with your chip, you'll want more power. Just prior to the chip, get your non-kicking foot ahead of the ball, if possible, and bring your kicking foot into position. Jam it under the center of the ball, again making contact with the ground in order to increase backspin. You may want to try to disguise this action so that the defending team doesn't see it coming and reacts slowly to the forward pass. Chipping a rolling ball is a harder skill as the ball is moving, so the last touch before the chip is vital. This touch needs to be a lighter one so that you can position your foot under the ball to get it up. See Chipping the Ball in the drill down section (page 162) for how to practice this skill.

COACH'S CORNER TIPS

Be where your feet are. Make sure that you are always focused on what is happening right now, and give "the now" your full attention.

MEET THE SOCCER STAR
JUDE BELLINGHAM

Birth Date: June 29, 2003

Position: Midfielder

Teams: Birmingham City, Borussia Dortmund, Real Madrid, and England

Jude Bellingham was born in the Midlands of England. After playing for his local club, Stourbridge Juniors, he joined Birmingham City as a U8 player. Jude developed in the Birmingham City program, and when he played his first game for the U23 team, he scored the winning goal in the 87th minute!

He left Birmingham to go to Germany where he played for Borussia Dortmund. He continued to set records, becoming the club's youngest goal scorer in a league game.

In June of 2023, Jude made his next move to LaLiga, Spain's top soccer league, to play for the Spanish giants Real Madrid. In his first season with Madrid, the team won the UEFA Champions League and Jude was named the Champions League Young Player of the Season.

On the field Jude Bellingham is a versatile midfielder who plays an attacking role. But he is just as good when playing as a defensive midfielder. His physical ability makes him a great player to help out his defensive line, and his strong understanding of the game can make it seem like he is in two places at once. As an attacking midfielder he has a wide range of passes that he uses to unbalance the opposition. He has a great ability to play a pass into a space where it looks like there is no space!

Jude has developed into a leader for his club team, and when he plays for the English National Team, he is a key player. If he plays well, his team has a better chance at winning!

LEVEL ① ❷ ③

Bending the Ball: Inside of Foot

TYPE OF TECHNIQUE: Passing, ball striking

PLAYER TO WATCH: David Beckham, player for Manchester United, Real Madrid, AC Milan, Paris Saint-Germain, LA Galaxy, and England

GAMES TO WATCH: Manchester United games (1992–2003)

PLAYER TO WATCH: Diego Maradona, player for Argentinos Juniors, Newell's, Boca Juniors, Barcelona, Napoli, and Argentina

GAMES TO WATCH: 1986 and 1990 World Cup Games

You've probably already learned a little about how to bend the ball. In this section we will talk about how to bring this skill into the game to help your team and open up the field.

Soccer is not a game of straight lines. Players don't just move up and down or across and back like foosball. We make bending runs, we cut inside and outside, we make passes that soar in the air and whip past players on the ground. We make angled passes that cut between defenders. Soccer truly is a "3D" game. If you can perfect the skill of bending the ball with the inside of your foot, then you will have yet another advanced weapon at your disposal.

Being able to bend the ball into the path of a teammate lets you play unexpected passes into the dangerous space behind the back line from any part of the field. It allows you to really punish the opponents if their defensive positioning is not well set up. You can play this type of pass from the center of the field to a wide player, and you can play this type of pass from wide positions to advanced players. We see this type of ball striking from many free kicks when players are trying to bend the ball around the wall into the goal, or up and over the wall and away from the keeper.

TRY IT

The ball bends because of what you do to it. You are in control. In order to bend the ball with the inside of your foot, you must connect on the outside of the ball to make it spin. When using your right foot, you want to spin the ball counterclockwise, and when using your left foot, you want the ball to spin clockwise.

Because you are hitting the ball on the outside, your non-kicking foot can be a little closer to the ball than it would be for a straight-line side-foot pass. This will help you get more spin on the ball. On contact, your toe should be up and your heel should be down with the ankle locked. The more speed you can generate with your kicking foot, the better, since that will increase spin. The more the ball spins, the more it bends. The key here is balance, because if you strike it with too much speed, you'll lose control. "Trial and error" is the name of the game. Practice, practice, practice.

COACH'S CORNER TIPS

Use self-talk to help your technique. Talk about your positioning and your action when the ball comes to you. For example, you can remind yourself of your steps from training. "Get my feet set, watch the ball come to my foot, relax my ankle joint, and control the ball."

LEVEL ① ② ❸

Bending the Ball: Outside of Foot

TYPES OF TECHNIQUE: Passing, ball striking

PLAYER TO WATCH: Roberto Carlos, player for Palmeiras, Inter Milan, Real Madrid, and Brazil

GAME TO WATCH: 1997 Tournoi de France, Brazil vs. France

Bending the ball with the outside of the foot is one of the most challenging skills in the game. Perfecting this skill will put you in the elite category of players in your age group. We see this type of ball striking in passing, in some free kicks, and in some shooting opportunities. This outer-foot ball-striking technique can be really challenging for goalkeepers to stop, because the ball looks like it is going away from them. It starts to curl into the post very late, and many times goalkeepers don't make an effort for the ball because they (mistakenly) think it's going wide. The joke is on them! (Do you see why this trick pass puts you in the elite category?)

As important as technique is with this pass, your pass selection is also key. Because it's a challenging skill, the chances of an error are a little higher. In order to give yourself the best chance for success, you must be well-balanced and in the correct body position to make this pass. Because of its difficulty, you might not want to use this technique at center field or in your own defending third until you have mastered it. Your decision-making and pass selection will improve over time, but you will most likely make some errors as you develop this skill. Be patient here.

TRY IT

Bending the ball is all about generating spin. When you are bending the ball with the outside of the foot, make contact with the inside of the ball, or the part of the ball that is closest to the center of the body. This connection will set the ball spinning. For outer-foot bends, the left-footed player wants to make the ball spin counterclockwise; right-footed players will be trying to get the ball to spin clockwise. When you are learning this difficult skill, it's best to hit a stationary ball and then progress to a moving ball. When using the outside of the foot, your non-kicking foot is placed a little behind the ball. This creates the space you need to strike the ball. Both feet need to be on the same side of the ball as the spot you hit—this is what makes this technique so difficult. On contact, your toe will be down and your ankle will be locked. You will make contact with the ball at the center line of the ball, but on the outside of the ball, to generate spin. If you imagine the ball as a clock with six o'clock in contact with the ground and twelve o'clock at the very top of the ball, then you are trying to make contact between the seven o'clock and eight o'clock spots with your right foot and between four o'clock and five o'clock spots with your left foot.

This is a challenging skill, so lots of practice will be required in order to master it. Keep at it. If you can perfect this technique, it will greatly improve your game. It will be worth it in the end! Be patient, as you may find it difficult to make the right shape with your foot. Don't worry about this; just keep working on it.

COACH'S CORNER TIPS

Keep your eyes and ears open after you make a mistake. Mistakes are good learning opportunities, so make sure you don't tune them out.

LEVEL

The L Turn

TYPE OF TECHNIQUE: Attacking, dribbling

PLAYER TO WATCH: Diego Maradona, player for Argentinos Juniors, Newell's, Boca Juniors, Barcelona, Napoli, and Argentina

GAME TO WATCH: 1986 World Cup quarterfinal, Argentina vs. England

The L turn looks like you pulled the ball backward behind you and passed it to yourself. It has two variations that allow you to either keep the ball on the same side of your body in the turn, or to transfer the ball to the other foot and turn in the other direction. Since you can turn to your left or right, the L turn allows you to change your decision mid-turn based on the reaction of the defenders.

This turn looks cool, it's pretty simple, and it's very effective. Focus on rolling the ball with the sole of your foot, because that will bring the defender in and create space for you to escape.

TRY IT

If you are left-footed, start with your foot on top of the ball. In the first part of the move, roll the ball forward with the sole of your foot, past your non-kicking foot. This movement will attract the defender to the ball. If you can exaggerate this movement, you will draw pressure and set up your opponent for the move. Now roll the ball backward, all the way past your non-kicking foot, so it's behind you. Essentially you have gone forward and backward with the ball, without releasing your foot. By keeping your foot on the ball, you are maintaining possession, and any contact from the defender will most likely draw a foul.

Now you have two choices: If pressure is coming toward you on your left (when the ball is under the left foot), roll the ball with the sole of your foot underneath you and behind your plant foot (the right foot in this case). Switch feet so your right foot has the ball. Did you catch that? You went forward and back with your left foot, never letting your foot off the ball; then when the ball was behind you, you tapped the ball behind you to your right foot. Quickly move off toward your right with the ball on your right foot. If the pressure is coming from your right when the ball is on your left foot, open up your body to 90 degrees and move away with the ball on your left foot by tapping it behind you. Of course, if you are getting pressure head-on, you can go either direction to escape. This move can also get you out of a tight spot if you are double-teamed, as long as you have an outlet to your left or right.

For the right-footed player, get your right foot on top of the ball. Now roll it forward and then backward past your plant foot. Exaggerating this movement will draw pressure and set up your opponent for the trick move. Look where the pressure is coming from and make your escape by either rolling the ball to your left, behind your left foot, and then taking the ball with your left foot into space, or by turning to your right 90 degrees and escaping to your right with the ball on your right foot.

Practice this move on your own, without an opponent. Once you feel you have it down pat, are comfortable with the ball behind you, and can quickly make the 90-degree turn, try it out with an opponent. See Ball Manipulation (page 164) for how to practice this skill.

COACH'S CORNER TIPS

Set small, achievable goals for yourself and you'll see your skills progress. Try to set a process goal every six weeks. For example, in the next six weeks, focus on improving your first-touch passing by getting your feet set early. Reassess after six weeks and set another goal.

LEVEL 1 2 3

The Step-Over Turn

TYPE OF TECHNIQUE: Attacking, dribbling

PLAYER TO WATCH: Neymar, player for Santos, Al Hilal, Barcelona, Paris Saint-Germain, and Brazil

GAME TO WATCH: 2016–2017 Champions League round of 16, Barcelona vs. Paris Saint-Germain

The step-over turn is a simple turn that allows you to buy yourself some space, change direction, and change the foot you are using—all at once. It can be used anywhere on the field, and is a simple trick to have up your sleeve (or in your socks!) as it will get you out of a tight spot. I call it the step-over turn, because you actually do step over the ball. What's important is the skill, which is a turn, as it gets you facing a different direction. You can start by walking through it with a smaller ball, maybe even a tennis ball, so that you can learn the movement pattern.

TRY IT

For the right-footed player, start with the ball on the right side. Approach the ball as if you are trying to play a pass behind the defender or play a pass down the touchline for a player to run onto. You are trying to make the defender think that it will be a hard pass and that you will be putting some force into the ball. As you go to strike the ball, your toe is down and your heel is up, as if you are about to pelt it.

Instead of striking the ball like the defender thinks you will, step over the outside of the ball with your right foot and land on the front half of your right foot. The ball is now on your right, with your whole body protecting it from the defender. As you land on your right foot, pivot your body around on your right foot, and bring your left foot around so that it lands close to the ball. You're now facing the opposite direction. The ball will be on your left side, with the defender now on your right. To complete the play, on the next touch with your left foot, take the ball into the empty space away from the defender. This may sound tricky, but it works like a charm at pace. You'll figure it out after you've practiced it a bit.

For the left-footed player, when the defender is on your left, plant your feet as if you were going to smack the ball with your left foot—but don't. You're only doing that to fake out the defender; it's a setup for the step-over turn you're about to do. As you go to strike the ball, step over the ball instead with your toe down and heel up, and land on the front half of your left foot. The ball is now all the way on your left and is protected from the defender by your whole body. You're facing the opposite direction. As you land on your left foot, pivot on your left toe and bring your right foot around; your left foot should land close to the ball. The ball is now on your right side, with the defender on the left, so the ball is well protected. To finish the play, use your right foot to take the ball into the open space you just created. Ta-da!

You should be able to do this turn on both sides of your body. It gets you turned in a different direction and allows you to switch feet at the same time. It happens quickly, catches the defense off guard, and is an impressive fake out.

COACH'S CORNER TIPS

Tracking your performance will help you see how far you've come. Set a performance goal for every four games you play in. An example could be decreasing the number of times you lose possession in your own half in a game. Tracking your progress will help you make better decisions on the field.

LEVEL ① ② ❸

The Scissors or Step-Over Move

TYPE OF TECHNIQUE: Attacking, dribbling

PLAYER TO WATCH: Cristiano Ronaldo, player for Sporting, Manchester United, Real Madrid, Juventus, Al-Nassr, and Portugal

GAME TO WATCH: 2006 World Cup, Portugal vs. France

You just learned about the step-over turn, which got you facing a different direction. That's why that's a turn. This skill is a move with a similar name since it will let you put a move on the defender in front of you and help you get past them. You can start with a smaller ball to learn the pattern, maybe a size 3 or size 4 ball, and then move up to a bigger ball when you are ready.

The scissors, sometimes also referred to as a step-over move, is a fast-paced skill that is meant to unbalance the opponent. Here, you use both feet and upper body to sell the move and get the defender off-balance. It happens quickly!

When you are doing the scissors, you have to get your upper body involved. You are trying to fake out the defender and get them to act on your first move. If you stay too upright on the first part, the defender may stay in their position, making things harder for you. In your approach to the defender, dribble right at them. This will help you stop their movement toward you and freeze them in place. Once you have stopped them, you can start the move and get them where you want them to go.

TRY IT

Make sure you have enough room in front of you; if the ball is right underneath your feet, odds are you'll trip and fall over yourself. Not exactly what we're going for here.

Start off with the ball in front of your stronger foot. If the ball is on your right side, start with your right foot on the inside of the ball and go around in a clockwise direction, toe down and heel up, until you land your right foot on the far side of the ball at two o'clock. If the ball is on your left, start the move with the left foot inside, toe down and heel up, moving counterclockwise and landing on the left foot at ten o'clock. As you land, get your shoulder over your foot—you want the defender to think you are moving to your strong side.

If the ball is on your right, your right foot just landed at two o'clock. Take your left foot and make contact with the ball at four o'clock. Flick the ball to the left with the outside of your left foot, toe down. It will head to the space on the left that the defender has moved away from, because they followed you to the right. If the ball is on your left, take your right foot and flick the ball with the outside of right your foot at eight o'clock, away from the defender. It will go to the now-empty space on the right. The defender thought you were going left, so they went the wrong way.

The final part of this move is to break after the ball and get the next touch on the ball as soon as possible. This is where the move pays off, and you go flying away with the ball.

COACH'S CORNER TIPS

You can use self-talk to motivate yourself by talking about what you can do and how you will do it. For example, before a game or training session, tell yourself, "I can score this penalty. I have done it before and I will do it again." This is a way to push yourself to rise to the moment. You can do it!

LEVEL ① ② ❸

The Cruyff Turn: The Total Fake Out

TYPE OF TECHNIQUE: Attacking, dribbling

PLAYER TO WATCH: Johan Cruyff, player for Ajax, Barcelona, Feyenoord, and the Netherlands

GAME TO WATCH: 1974 World Cup, Netherlands vs. Sweden

It's no surprise that the Cruyff turn is named after its inventor, the great Dutch player Johan Cruyff. It first came to the world stage in the 1974 World Cup, when Cruyff unleashed it onto an unsuspecting Swedish defender. Essentially this is what we call a "dummy," where the player in possession fakes an action and then does something different. For example, a player could make it look like they're going to pass the ball forward, but once the opponent moves to block in the forward space, the player pulls the ball behind them and turns in the other direction. As with any successful trick, the key is to "sell" the move to the defender with exaggerated movements, to get them into the position you want them (the direction you aren't going in!). This leaves the defender scrambling to catch up to the player with the ball, or pulls other defenders off their marks, leaving another player open to receive a pass.

You can do this move in many different parts of the field, but it has its greatest impact when performed in wide positions **higher up the field**, since the first part of the move is the faking of a cross with your stronger foot.

If you can perfect the Cruyff turn, then you always have a trick that allows you to beat a defender at a time when you might look like you are in trouble, such as when you are being forced away from goal. This trick is the hardest one to defend against, because the defender has to try to stop the cross, and by doing so, they open the door for you.

TRY IT

With your back to the goal line and the defender inside, push the ball away from you. As you come to the ball, set up as if you're going to play a long cross with your strong foot, the one farthest away from the defender. As you make contact with the ball, flick it back underneath you, in between your plant foot and your kicking foot. Now you can attack the goal line and goal, as you have beaten your defender. You can use either foot, since you are in the clear.

Let's slow it down a bit. To start the move, you need the ball on the foot that is farthest away from the defender. Let's say that you are wide on the left with the ball on your left side, and the defender is on the inside. Push the ball forward as if you were about to make a cross with your left foot. Get your plant foot in place, which will be just behind the ball, and wind up to make the cross. As the defender goes to block the cross, bring the ball back with your left big toe between your kicking foot and your plant foot, and head into the space that the defender just left open (because they set up to block what they thought was your cross). You have to really sell the cross, because you want the defender to stretch to block it. Now you can come back onto the ball with either foot, since you have created a space to go into. This will bring you inside and into free space.

The best use of the Cruyff turn is in a wide position when you are closely marked, have your back to the goal line, and are moving away from the goal line. This is how Cruyff first introduced the turn. This move is best operated by a right-footed player on the left wing and a left-footed player on the right wing; so if you find yourself in those areas, this is a great option for you.

This is a challenging skill, and you need to be patient when practicing. Try this on your own, but in order to perfect this skill, you need to try it on an opponent, so be prepared for a few failures at first. Once you get it, though, you will become a difficult opponent to beat!

COACH'S CORNER TIPS

Try to avoid setting outcome goals. You are not fully in control of any outcome. If your goal is to win the game, recognize that you can't win it on your own. Even if you and your team played the best game possible, you could still lose. Focus on your progress as a player.

The Matthews Move: A Ball Dance

LEVEL ① ❷ ③

TYPE OF TECHNIQUE: Attacking, ball control, dribbling

PLAYER TO WATCH: Stanley Matthews, player for Stoke City, Blackpool, and England

GAME TO WATCH: Matthews's career finished in 1965, so it's very hard to find a clip of him performing his own move. You can search the Matthews move online and find a good example, though.

This superfast move is named after famous English player Sir Stanley Matthews. (Bet you could have figured part of that out.) Matthews was the Ronaldo of his day, roasting fullbacks every week in the English league. His signature move was a quick movement that changed his foot position from the outside of his foot contacting the outside of the ball, to the inside of his foot making contact with the inside of the ball. This move unbalances defenders. You want to try to draw them into going for the ball and then push the ball past them into open space. The key to taking your foot from outside to inside of the ball is to make sure that your toe is down and your heel is up when you flick the ball.

This slick trick can be used at pace or when you have a defender isolated, like in wide positions. You can slow the defender down, slow the game down, and then get away at speed—and look cool while doing it.

TRY IT

In open play, this is a fast move meant to deceive the defender. If you are right-footed, push the ball with the inside of your right foot lightly, at four o'clock. Get the defender to move a little toward you and the ball. You are trying to make it look like you are just moving the ball to your left, and not sure of your next move. (But, hah! You sure do know your next move.) At that moment, you have created open space on the right, because the defender thinks you are moving to the left. As you release your right foot from the ball, quickly move your right foot to eight o'clock with your toe down and heel up, and flick the ball to your right (the defender's left). Break into the space on the right that you created with your first small touch. See you later, defender!

For the left-footed player, the ball is on your inside, with the defender in front of you. A small touch with the inside of the left foot, at eight o'clock on the ball, brings the defender toward you. The defender thinks you are going to kick to the right, which creates a space on your left. As you release, quickly take your left foot to the inside of the ball, at four o'clock, with the toe down, and flick the ball back to the left into the space you just created. Nice work!

This is a great move for a wide player when you have the defender isolated. If you can approach the defender at around 45 degrees, then when you break with the outside of the foot, you will be moving toward the goal line and in a good position to make a cross for your team.

The Matthews move is a good one to unbalance your opponent. You can start by using a smaller ball and go slowly to learn the pattern, then build up the speed of the movement when you are ready.

COACH'S CORNER TIPS

Remember that you are not your performance. Treat winning and losing the same—don't get too high after a win or too low after a loss. We all have good days and bad days.

PART 3

Strategies

If technique is all about you, then strategy is all about the team. Strategy is how to play your part to help your team perform at their best and hopefully win some games. We use strategies to help us gain an advantage in the competitive environment we play in. Very often our strategies are built around the strengths of our team and its players. If we have some fast players, we may decide to defend a little deeper and hit our opponent on the break by using long passes for our speedsters to run onto. We may also decide to build our strategy around some of our weaknesses by trying to protect areas where we are not as strong. For example, maybe our two fullbacks are injured, and the players coming in are inexperienced. In this instance, our strategy might be to play with three center backs and position those less experienced fullbacks a little higher.

Whatever we plan, the key is to all be on the same page. If we are defending high up, then our midfielders and strikers need to be prepared and ready to go. If we are playing on the break, then we need our speedsters to stay inside and be ready to make runs into space when we win the ball. Soccer *is* a team game, and if you know what everyone is doing and when they are doing it, you will become a key member of the team.

LEVEL 1 2 3

Receiving The Ball

TYPE OF STRATEGY: Offense and defense attacking, receiving the ball, decision-making

PLAYERS TO WATCH: Xavi, player for Barcelona, Al Sadd, and Spain; Andrés Iniesta, player for Barcelona, Vissel Kobe, Emirates,and Spain

GAME TO WATCH: 2011 Champions League Final, Barcelona vs. Manchester United

When your team is in possession, you must be able to take part in the movement and build up play, regardless of your position or role in the team. More often than not, when you receive the ball, you will have to make a decision about what to do with it on your very first touch. The earlier you can decide, the better, because that will give you time to prepare and get your feet in the right place. Then it's time to execute and let your technique take over.

A colleague and an excellent coach named Rob Csabai calls this situation "pin it, push it, or pass it." What this means is that, when the ball comes to you, those are the only three options: You can pin the ball to you, which draws pressure to the ball and potentially opens up spaces in other areas. You can push the ball into space, which opens up the game for you to then look at areas in front of you. Or you can pass the ball first touch to a teammate in order to keep the ball moving. There isn't one right answer here, or one preferred choice. You simply have to make a decision based on where you are and what you see.

TRY IT

If you want to pin the ball in the space in front of you, you can use two parts of your foot to do this. You want to stop the ball in front of you in order to draw pressure to the ball. Of course,

you need to make sure you have an escape route as the defender approaches you! When the ball comes to you, you can choose to trap the ball with the sole of your foot and stop it dead, or you can use the side of your foot and wedge the ball between your foot and the ground.

If you want to push the ball into space, then as the ball comes to you, get in a position where you can use either the inside of your foot to control the ball into space or the outside of your foot to take the ball into the area you want to move into. The difference between these two connections with the ball is the shape and direction of your foot: When you use the inside of your foot, the toe is up with the heel down. Your foot could also be in a flat position, where the sole of your foot runs parallel to the ground when you use the outside of your foot.

If you want to pass the ball first touch, then an early decision will allow you to get in position, get set, and focus on contact. A good first-touch pass gives the next player time and space in order to keep the play going.

As you can see, the difficulty level changes if opponents are near you when you receive the ball. Don't worry about the opponent. Focus on your job and be aware of your surroundings.

COACH'S CORNER TIPS

Always focus on your decisions and your role on the team. Some questions to think about during a game or training session are: Where is the ball? Am I in the right place? What will I do with the ball? Where is my next pass? This is called tactical self-talk.

Helping the Player with the Ball

TYPE OF STRATEGY: Offense and defense attacking, offering support to the ball carrier

PLAYER TO WATCH: Ousmane Dembélé, player for Borussia Dortmund, Barcelona, Paris Saint-Germain, and France

GAME TO WATCH: 2025 Champions League Final, Paris Saint-Germain vs. Inter Milan

Soccer is a simple game, often made complicated by coaches and players! As you know, the general idea is to score more goals than your opponent. In order to do that, you need the ball. If you don't have it, you have to get it back. When you do have it, you have to make your possession count.

In order to keep the ball and create a scoring chance, you must support the player in possession. If you leave them isolated with the ball, they will be challenged before too long. Without support, there is a good chance they will lose the ball, and you will have to win it back again. (Having said that, there are times when you should consider *not* supporting the player on the ball, since it may bring extra defenders close to the ball. We will look at that soon in Breaking Lines on page XXX.)

When you make runs to support the player on the ball, you must make the commitment to get to your teammate as fast as possible. You also have to accept the fact that you may not get the ball—and it's not your fault. Offering support changes the picture around the ball, and other options may open up by the time you get there. Be prepared to not get the ball. Go anyway! Think about this: The one time you decide not to make that supporting run may be the key moment in the game!

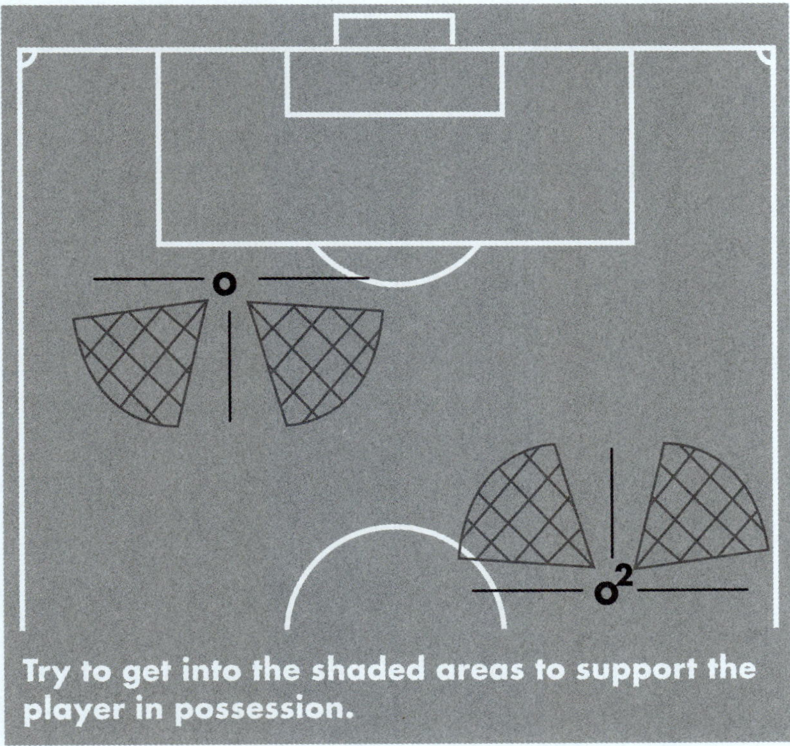

Try to get into the shaded areas to support the player in possession.

TRY IT

Before we talk about how and when to support a player on the ball, let's discuss something that is rarely encouraged: when *not* to go in close. If a teammate receives the ball and is in a 1v1 situation against a defender, unless you can offer support without bringing another defender with you, leave your teammate alone in the 1v1 situation.

The other time to consider staying out of the way is if a teammate has possession and has space behind the defender to attack. Stay away, and don't fill that space or bring extra defenders with you, because that would limit the options for your teammate. Let them decide what the right play should be. They can always call you over if they need help beating the defender.

The only time you should think about supporting them is if you can make it a 2v1 in your team's favor. When you commit to supporting the player on the ball, think about the angle and speed of your approach. If you get there too late, your teammate could have lost the ball. If you get there too early, you bring extra pressure close to the ball.

When supporting your teammate with the ball, think about where you want to finish your run. Where can you best support the ball carrier? Try to get in a position on an angle so that your teammate has to send you an angled pass. Try to find a space that isn't on a horizontal or vertical line with your teammate. **Square passes** can be easily intercepted. Vertical passes make it harder to play one touch. Angled passes are much better and easier to work with.

You will see the different difficulty levels for this skill. Level 1: When the ball is in your own half, there are going to be more of your players around, so you should find it easier to get to a spot to support the player with the ball. Level 2: When you are in your opponent's half, you will probably be outnumbered, so you have to work a little harder to find the right spot to support your teammate.

COACH'S CORNER TIPS

Be positive and speak to your strengths. Don't doubt yourself! Some things you can tell yourself during a training session or a game are: "I am good at passing the ball." "My opponent does not have my technique." "I am fast and I will get to the ball first." "I am the hardest-working person in training, and I will set the tone for my team."

Recognizing Patterns in Play

LEVEL 1 **2** 3

TYPE OF STRATEGY: Offense and defense attacking and defending, spatial awareness, ball tracking

PLAYER TO WATCH: Lamine Yamal, player for Barcelona and Spain

GAME TO WATCH: 2025 Champions League semifinal, Barcelona vs. Inter Milan

Soccer is one of the most seemingly random games in the world, with many moving parts and a big space to play in. When a player has possession, there are many different things that can happen, with many different outcomes. When a pass is made and received, the next player will also have a similar number of options. Soccer produces a different game every time it is played. If you go to see a movie on Tuesday evening and then go back to see that movie again two weeks later, you will see the exact same movie. The events stay the same, each frame is in the same order, the actors are the same, and the outcome never changes. If you go watch a local soccer game, though, and then go and watch the same teams play two weeks later, you will see a different game. The same is true of your favorite professional team playing at the highest level of the sport. A team playing in one round of the World Cup, Champions League, Olympics, or other tournament will play a different game from the next round, and the next round and the next, even if the players don't change. The goal kicks, throw-ins, goals, fouls, corners, shots, etc., will all be in a different, random order—but they will still be there.

As a player, you need to be able to assess the seeming randomness of it all and figure out which events are closely linked. That way you can try to anticipate what will happen next. We call this skill "pattern recognition." We know that experts in all sports have excellent pattern recognition. They are able to remember many patterns and very quickly sort through their memory to recognize those patterns on the field as the game is being played. It helps them predict what will happen next and be ready for it. This is a learnable skill; it just takes time.

TRY IT

These tips will help you know what to do, but you can only put them into play by playing live.

Awareness is most important. Looking up and around allows you to be aware of developments in three areas. You know where the ball is at all times, and who has it. You can see the space around the ball, which includes the four to six players closest to the ball. And you can also see away from the ball, which includes the rest of the players on the field.

When your team has the ball, you should always be taking your **cues** from the ball carrier; they are the one in charge of the situation. Make sure you can always see their hips, because that will give you a sense of what direction the next play might be in. Try to get a look at their feet to predict what play they might be setting up for. The distance between their feet will indicate whether they are planning to play a short or longer pass, or whether they are going to keep the ball. The more you can take in visually, the better decisions you can make.

This keen awareness applies to watching your opponents as well. If you can predict what they might do, you can already be in place when it happens. When your team is defending and your opponents outnumber you, stay focused on the bigger picture.

Since it's too hard to play man-to-man, start to make your way to where you think the ball will be passed. If you're already in position, you can either intercept a pass or close that area off.

The best players in the world have this ability to pick up patterns before others and to always find themselves in the right place. If you get a chance to go to see a game, then take the time to watch the best players and see how they move around the field. They never go where the ball is—they go to where the ball is going.

COACH'S CORNER TIPS

Imagery is what we see in our head when we close our eyes. Like self-talk, we can use imagery to build confidence and motivate ourselves for the game by imagining our successful performance.

LEVEL 1 2 3

Living in the Triangle

TYPES OF STRATEGIES: Offense and defense attacking, finding space

PLAYER TO WATCH: Xavi, player for Barcelona, Al Sadd, and Spain

GAME TO WATCH: 2012 Euro Final, Spain vs. Italy

The triangle is any space on the field between three of your opponents. Living in the triangle means having the confidence to go into that space in an attempt to get possession of the ball. Of course, there will be times in the game when there are no triangles to be filled. If you are playing high up the field, for example, and your opponents are defending close to their own goal, finding these spaces will be difficult.

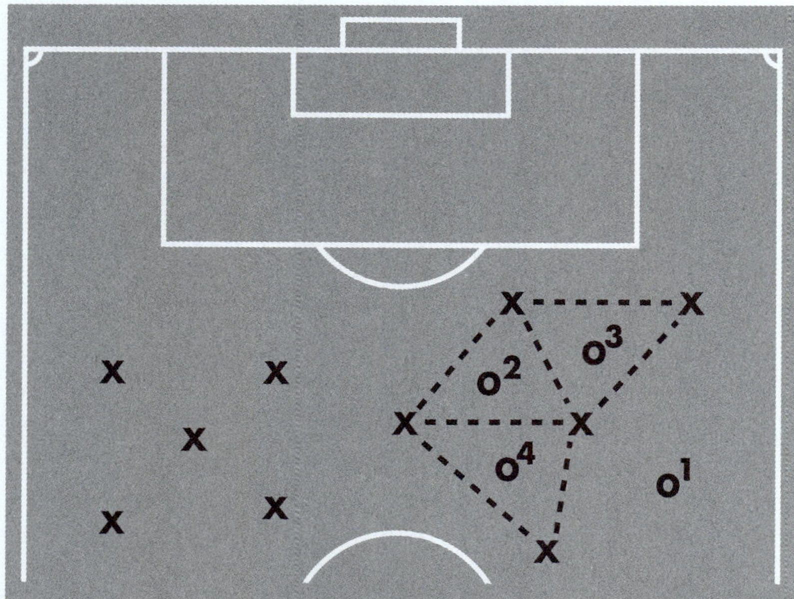

Player O1 is not a threat to the opponents. Players O2, O3 and O4 live inside a triangle. If they receive the ball they will be a threat to the opponent.

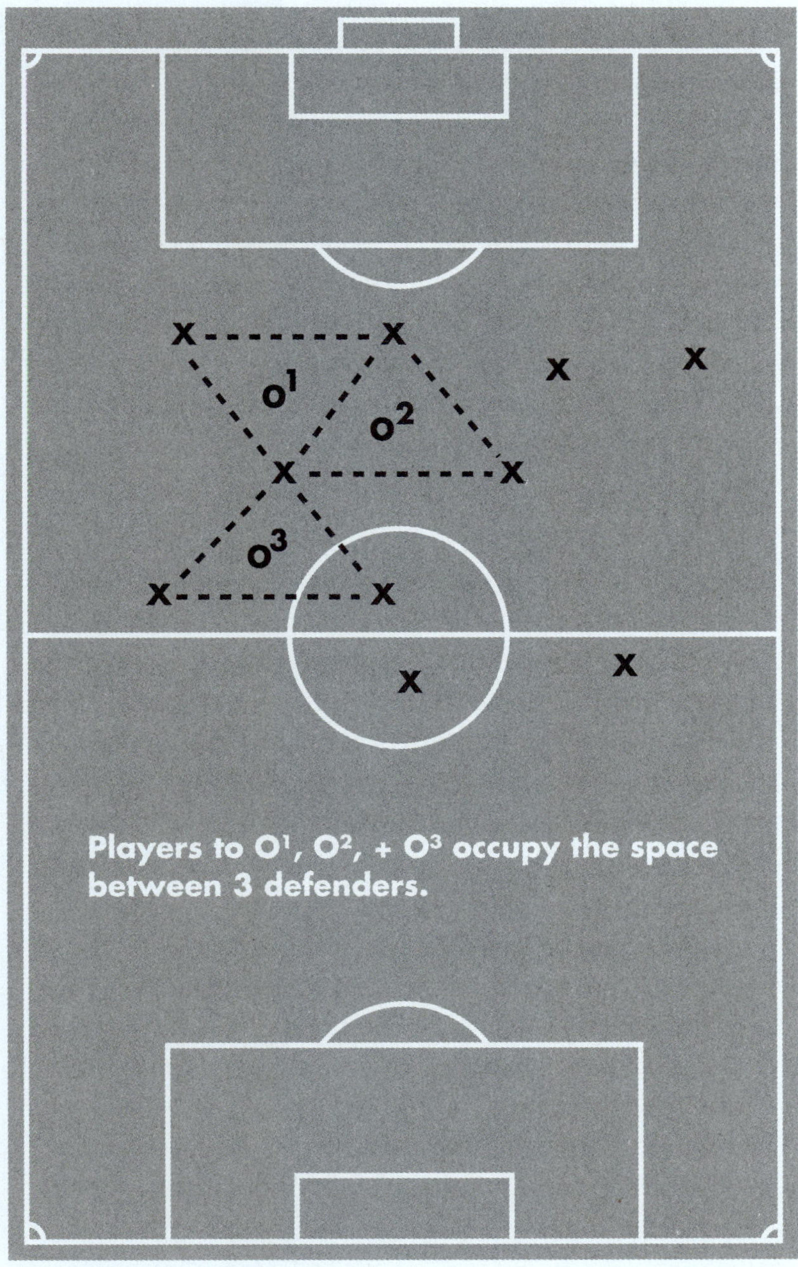
X
X
O1
O2
X
X
X
X
O3
X
X
X
X
Players to O1, O2, + O3 occupy the space between 3 defenders.

Living in the triangle is another way of disrupting the opponent and making them react to your ball movement and possession, so the timing of your movement into the triangle is important. If you move into the space too soon, you could "kill the space." Your opponent will react to your movement and cut you off from the ball, therefore shutting down any chance of building an attack through that area. If you make a move into a triangle as the ball is moving in a different direction, then you are filling a dead space and not really helping your team or the ball carrier. Finding the right time to go into and live in that key space can be challenging, but it can be learned.

TRY IT

You don't always have to receive the ball when you are living in the triangle to help your team. If you get into the space at the right time, that movement alone will disrupt your opponent and help the player on the ball. The time to enter the triangle is when the ball carrier has time on the ball and is able to see different options. At this point, look at the positions that your opponents are in to find the triangle. Then move into it. As long as the defenders are more than six yards apart, you can fill that space. Move into the space and keep your feet moving. If a defender comes closer to mark you, then start to move away from the ball carrier in order to take that defender away from the ball. The bigger the space, the longer you can stay in it. As the play develops, you'll need to move out of the space and find another supporting position.

As you move in and occupy the space, try to find a quick option so that if you don't get a good pass, you can play the ball either back to the player who passed you the ball or out of the triangle with one touch. If you get the ball under control, then hold the ball and engage one of your other three players from

the triangle. Ideally, you'll move the opponent and keep the ball moving forward.

The difference in difficulty level is based on where the triangle is. If you are in your own half, then there is a good chance that you will find it easier to get into the triangle. When you're in the opponent's half, this will become harder, because they will have more defenders around you and they will find it easier to mark you.

COACH'S CORNER TIPS

You can use imagery to help you prepare for your games. Think about the field where you'll be playing. Have you played there before, or is it a new place for you? See yourself preparing to play. You are ready to go! Now imagine the first few minutes of the game and your first successful touches, runs, and challenges.

MEET THE SOCCER STAR
NAOMI GIRMA

Birth Date: June 14, 2000

Position: Central defender

Teams: San Diego Wave, Chelsea, and the United States

Naomi Girma was born in San Jose, California. She first played soccer for Maleda Soccer Club, where she was coached by her father. She then moved to Central Valley Crossfire before she was invited into the U.S. Soccer Women's U14 camp.

Naomi played collegiate soccer at Stanford University. In her sophomore year, she became team captain and led her team to the third National Championship. Naomi was named the Most Outstanding Defender of the tournament, PAC-12 Defender of the Year, and was First Team All-American.

Naomi was selected first in the 2022 NWSL draft by the San Diego Wave. In her first season, she was named Rookie of the Year and Defender of the Year, the first player in history to win both awards in the same season. And she made history again in 2025 when Chelsea FC paid over $1 million for Naomi to play for them. This made her the first million-dollar women's soccer player.

At the international level Naomi is the first player of Ethiopian descent to represent the U.S. In the Paris 2024 Olympics she played every minute of every game as the U.S. won the gold medal.

Naomi is already considered one of the best defenders in world football. She is known for her composure and coolness on the ball. She is able to read the game and anticipate where to be in order to help get the ball back. She is comfortable with the ball at her feet and is able to start attacks for her team as well as stop them!

LEVEL

Breaking Their Lines

TYPES OF STRATEGIES: Offense and defense attacking, passing, movement

PLAYER TO WATCH: Kevin De Bruyne, player for Genk, Chelsea, Werder Bremen, VfL Wolfsburg, Manchester City, Napoli, and Belgium

GAMES TO WATCH: 2023 Manchester City vs. Arsenal, 2024 Euro Belgium vs. Romania

As you move to the bigger field, breaking lines becomes a little more challenging. More space doesn't always make things easier. With more space comes more opponents who work together to cover those lines, so your passes and runs must still be well timed and into the best space.

By now you will know that your team, like everyone else, plays in lines: a back line, a group of midfielders that could be one or two lines, and a forward line. You may also have another line that you start defending from, which is sometimes called the line of confrontation. For example, that could be the halfway line. Often you will hear coaches tell their defenders to "hold the line." They are referring to the imaginary line that the defenders don't drop behind. While there are many lines in soccer, here we are talking about breaking and playing between the opponent's lines.

We can **break lines** with passes. A pass can get the ball past their line of defense before our players pass their line of defense. This happens most frequently, since there are always spaces between players to pass the ball between their lines. Square passes, or passes across the field, can help us keep possession; however, to create goal-scoring chances, we need forward passes.

In this example, the line of defenders is broken and at the same time the offside line is also broken. The player who makes this pass (O[1]) needs to be able to see the wide player (O[2]) so that they can time that pass. If the pass is too late or the run is made early, then the wide player will be offside and the team then loses possession.

1 O^1 passes to O^2, breaking the line between two opponents.

2 O^3 breaks the line with the ball between two opponents.

3 O^4 runs, breaks the line, and receives the ball from O^5.

You can also break lines with runs off the ball. This is an excellent way of disrupting and challenging your opponent. For example, if you are in a wide position, then a simple run down the line will put you between the opponent's midfielders and their defenders. You have broken one line and created an opportunity for a pass that breaks another one. Simple movements can produce big rewards when executed correctly.

You can also break lines by playing between their lines when you stay in the "triangle." See Living in the Triangle (page 74) for how to practice this strategy.

TRY IT

Breaking lines by playing between them will cause the most disruption to your opponent. As soon as you pop into the space between the lines, a question is asked of the opponent: Who is picking you up? Does a defender come forward or does a midfielder drop back? Whichever one they choose, you have disrupted their lines. Now your team can create an overload in an area of the field.

The keys to this movement are spatial awareness, timing, and confidence. As the game is developing, you need to have awareness of where players are positioned and where the spaces are that you can exploit. The only way to do this is by looking around and constantly checking around you. Some coaches call this "head on a swivel," and that is exactly what you need! Space doesn't appear; you have to be looking for it.

Once you have found the space, pick the right time to fill it. Make a move into the space as the player on the ball is ready to play the ball. If you move too soon and the pass is rushed, you will be covered. The key is to get between the lines and arrive just before the ball. Then the fun starts! You must have confidence in your ability to go into tight spaces and receive the ball. By doing this, you are helping your team. Sure, you will lose the ball at times. It's all part of learning the game. Find their lines and have the courage to break them.

COACH'S CORNER TIPS

Seeing yourself in the action helps you play a smarter game. See your best moments in the game, your pass that leads to a goal, and the winning goal you score after a successful dribble. If you can see it, you can achieve it!

LEVEL ① ② ❸

Breaking the Press

TYPE OF STRATEGY: Defense attacking, decision-making

PLAYER TO WATCH: Alexis Mac Allister, player for Argentinos Juniors, Brighton, Liverpool, and Argentina

GAMES TO WATCH: 2022 World Cup games featuring Argentina

The press, or **pressing**, is a style of defending that calls for the defending team to try to outnumber the team in possession in order to win the ball back. Pressing is not something that a team can do for long periods of time, because it takes high levels of energy. It is usually triggered by something that happens on the field.

For example, if your team has a throw-in in your own half, then that is an opportunity for the opponent to press that ball. Your team has a player off the field taking the throw, and it's far enough away from the opponent's goal for the opponent to be confident enough to commit players to the ball. If you receive a pass that is played behind you and you are then facing your own goal in possession, that is also a trigger that can be used to start pressing the ball. If one of your teammates plays a long ball that takes too much time to get to its destination, that can be a trigger for your opponents to press the ball, too.

Basically, whenever you receive the ball and it is hard to control, either because it is bouncing to you or between thigh height and head height, it can be used as an opportunity to press the ball. You need to know what these triggers are so that you can see the press coming. The sooner you pick up on the press, the more information you have in order to try to break down the opponents.

TRY IT

If you find yourself in any of the situations that will trigger your opponent to press, the first thing to do is stay calm. Your opponent can't press for long, because they don't have the levels of energy to keep the pace up for more than 20 to 30 seconds. Once you anticipate the press, make sure you get your head up so that you can see where they are coming from. Quickly figure out where you can escape to or pass to in order to break the press. Often the first player that comes in to challenge you will be coming in fast—but fast doesn't always equal good. If you can take advantage of their inability to slow down and get past the first pressuring defender, that may break the press in one move.

If you decide that you can't evade the first player, the next best option is a longer pass to where the *opponent* is outnumbered by *your* team. If the opponent is sending players to the ball, they are going to be shorthanded somewhere. Find out where. That is your destination. If you get there in one pass, fantastic. But the key is to not get the ball taken from you or have a pass intercepted. Stay calm, trust your technique, and be confident in your ability to break the press.

If you show the ability in games to break a press, it's safe to say that the opponents will stop pressing you. And you'll become a huge asset to your team.

COACH'S CORNER TIPS

See the outcome you're aiming for. See yourself in the last few minutes of the game. You're still running strong and your opponents are out of gas! The whistle blows, the game is over, and your team has played well and won. See the celebrations and congratulations. How does that feel? Now you are ready to play!

LEVEL ① ❷ ③

Zonal Marking

TYPE OF STRATEGY: Defending as a team, organization

TEAM TO WATCH: Liverpool (2015–2024), coach Jürgen Klopp

The idea behind zonal marking is that when your team is defending, you take up a defensive shape where each player is allocated a zone to fill. As the ball moves across the field, the team moves as a group and so do the zones. The focus is on spacing between players and the angles you take up in relation to one another. As you know, defending on angles is key so you don't get caught in a **square position** in relation to your defensive partners.

As a player on the team, it probably isn't your call as to whether you defend zonally or man-to-man. But that doesn't mean that you shouldn't have a good understanding of what these ideas are, how they work, and the strengths and weaknesses of these systems.

TRY IT

When you are involved in a zonal defense, your focus and concentration must be on playing in your zone. You need to be aware of what is in front of you, and who is coming into and out of your zone. Make sure that as opponents leave your zone, you are communicating with the teammate next to you so they know someone is moving into their space. There will be times when your zone gets overloaded. This means that the opponents will send two players into your zone. In this case, you need to be aware of where the ball is and what the player on the ball is doing. If you think the ball is coming your way, you will need to communicate with your teammates to get some help. If it looks like the ball won't be coming near you, then you can make the decision to deal with the two players in your zone at that time.

This helps because it will result in your team being able to overload a zone that may be closer to the ball.

When zonal marking works, it's a beautiful thing. In general, the opposition becomes so frustrated in their inability to break you down that they make poor decisions and give you the ball back. The keys to good zonal marking are organization, patience, awareness, cue recognition, and confidence in your team's ability to work together. When an opposition player enters your zone, they become your responsibility. As they move around and leave your zone, it's your job to tell teammates that they are coming and make sure your teammates are aware of what is happening.

There will be times when your zone becomes overloaded by the opponent. This often occurs when the ball is farther away from you. Your job here is to control your nerves and decide which player is the biggest threat. If you can manage two opponents in your zone, the chances for your team to get the ball back increase.

At all times, make sure you can see the ball, your opponent, and the space that they are trying to expose. If you can do this, you've done your job. You'll be in a good position, and the ball most likely won't come your way!

It takes some time to figure out zonal marking as a group. You have to be prepared for some mistakes, especially when moving players around due to injury, when bringing in new players, or when players leave the squad. It may take some time to adjust, so this might not work great right off the bat.

Zonal marking isn't the best way to mark when defending corners. The main reason is that you are waiting in your zone, standing still, and the opponent is usually charging in and jumping for the ball. This isn't a great situation to be in.

There is also a soft spot in zonal marking that can be a bit of a problem. It's the areas between the zones, what we might call the "seams," like the seams of a jacket. The area between two zones could be in both zones, or it might not be in either zone. Good opponents have a habit of finding these seams and causing nightmares. In this situation, someone on the team has to step up and be the leader, making the decisions as to who marks who, and for how long.

COACH'S CORNER TIPS

Manage your intensity level. If it's too low, you risk underperforming because you are not ready to play. If you are too intense, you can feel stress, anxiety, and panic, and this will affect your performance. Find the right level of intensity for you.

Man-to-Man Marking

TYPE OF STRATEGY: Defense speed, anticipation

PLAYER TO WATCH: Michael Essien, player for Bastia, Lyon, Chelsea, Real Madrid, AC Milan, and Ghana

GAMES TO WATCH: Chelsea (2008–2009)

PLAYER TO WATCH: N'Golo Kanté, player for Boulogne, Caen, Leicester City, Chelsea, Al-Ittihad, and France

GAME TO WATCH: 2021 Champions League Final, Chelsea vs. Manchester City

The idea behind man-to-man marking is pretty much as it sounds: As a defender, you are assigned to play against a specific opponent. That is the player you mark and stick with. I hope you are thinking that this would be a challenge to sustain throughout the whole game and field. If you are, that's good; it's fair to say that it would not only be difficult to do, but it would also turn out to be a disaster. You would have to win the vast majority of 50–50 balls, all around the field, in order to have any success. That's not easy to do, especially if the other player is more advanced. Don't worry; this strategy is usually only employed for short periods of time, or in certain locations.

With man-to-man marking, you want to be about one to two arm lengths away from your opponent. Any farther away and you allow them space to receive the ball. Any closer and you can't react to a quick change of direction. You will find the right spot, but be prepared to be wrong before you get it right.

TRY IT

Man-to-man marking is mostly employed from corners or free kicks from wide positions that will be crossed into your 18. Man-to-man marking is also used to "man mark" the opponent's most dangerous player. Very often in this style of marking, there is a combination of man marking and zonal play, where your team may have two players who will mark their star player based on where they are when they receive that ball.

When you are in this style of defending, your focus should be on the player that you are lined up against. In particular, for corners or free kicks, it's important that you position yourself where you can close down this player very quickly. But make sure you don't get too close, since you might lose them in the movement of the game. It's not uncommon to see a **basketball pick** employed in these situations, so make sure that you avoid the traffic and keep a clear line of sight between you and the player you are matched up against.

From corners, man-to-man marking allows you to get the physical matchups, mostly in terms of height, that allow you to have the best chance of winning the first contact on the ball. Defensively, getting that first contact on the ball is vital, because it disrupts any patterns that the opponent has been working on.

Sometimes you have a player—and this may be you—that just takes to man-to-man marking and really enjoys the challenge. Having the ability to track a player and not get beaten by them is rare. If you can develop this part of your game, you will become a player of interest to many coaches.

You can't go man-to-man for long periods of time or play it close to your own goal, because it's simply too risky. The best players are able to lose their markers and play in between the lines, which disrupts any opportunity of long-term man-to-man marking. The game of soccer is just too fluid and played on too big a space to even think about only using man-to-man marking. As you move to the bigger field, this will become much more obvious!

When you are engaged in man-to-man marking, the biggest issue is getting the matchups correct. Physical matchups are important, but the real danger is speed. Speed kills, and if you can't match up your fastest defender with their fastest attacker, something bad is going to happen! When the marked player breaks free, who will leave their marked player to go and confront the ball carrier?

COACH'S CORNER TIPS

Use some high-energy music and slow deep breaths to help you raise your intensity for the game. Deep breathing will reduce your stress level and defeat anxiety.

LEVEL

③

Defending from the Front Line

TYPES OF STRATEGIES: Defending as a team, communication, organization, decision-making

TEAM TO WATCH: Spain's Men's National Team 2000–2010

The idea of defending high up the field and leaving space behind you can be a little frightening. No defender likes leaving their goalkeeper to fend for themselves. If your group of defenders all head toward the center line, it leaves your team vulnerable. If your opponent gets the ball past your team, they can create goal-scoring opportunities, particularly if they have some fast players up front. Of course, the opposite argument is that the closer you are to the opponent's goal when you win possession, the shorter the distance you have to travel in order to score a goal for your team. Both sides of this coin are true, but they are missing the real point. The key to defending from the front line is to make sure you're committed to winning the ball high up the field. You need to be strategic about how you do it.

When defending from the front, ideally you want to have four players in your attacking third when the opponents have a goal kick. However, you don't want these players tightly marking the opposition's defenders. If you do that, your opponent will most likely look to play the ball over those players, into the midfield area. You will most likely be outnumbered there, since you committed your players higher up the field near the goalkeeper. You want your players in positions that are just a little higher than the normal starting positions when defending a goal kick. Players should be on the **front foot** and ready to start closing down the player who is receiving the ball. As you may know, the new goal kick rule encourages teams to try and play out from a goal kick. If you are organized, you can use this rule change to your advantage.

TRY IT

As the ball is played, your team needs to start preparing for action. Your team's mantra should be "get together and stay together." As the ball leaves the 18, your focus should be on applying immediate but controlled pressure to the ball carrier. You need a player to dart out and close down the ball carrier and not dive into a challenge to win the ball, since another one of your players is coming to help.

From a team perspective, as soon as your second player arrives to help out, your team can all move forward as a group and take up advanced positions. This is the "get together" part. Success for your team is to stop the forward motion of your opponent. Now you need to focus on the "stay together" part. Communication is the key. Your pressuring players need to know where to force the play and when they can safely challenge for the ball.

COACH'S CORNER TIPS

Use this mental checklist for a good warm-up: Make sure you have lots of body movements in the physical warm-up, do a mental rehearsal of your game, think of some key words to help you stay focused, and check your intensity level.

LEVEL 1 2 **3**

Defending Against Their Playmaker

TYPE OF STRATEGY: Defense, marking

PLAYERS TO WATCH: Park Ji-sung, player for Kyoto Purple Sanga, PSV Eindhoven, Manchester United, Queens Park Rangers, and South Korea; Andrea Pirlo, player for Brescia, Inter Milan, Reggina, AC Milan, Juventus, New York City FC, and Italy

GAME TO WATCH: 2010 Champions League, Manchester United vs. AC Milan

Man marking, or shadowing your opponent's best player, is not something that we hear too much about. Many teams have a defensive plan that they stick to. If this works for the team, then it's a smart thing to do. When you are assigned to mark a player in a 1v1 situation, there are two parts to the puzzle.

First of all, are you mentally up to the challenge? Can you accept that you probably won't win every battle with your opponent? If they outrun or outplay you, will you still have the confidence to go up against them the next time they get the ball? I am sure you have heard that you don't have to win every battle to win the war. This is certainly true in a game of soccer. What is more important is what battles you choose to fight and where you choose to fight them. You don't need to chase someone all over the field all day long; you just need to beat them in the right places at the right times. Experience is how you'll figure out what to play and what to leave alone; it's not something that can be written down. Every game and every player is different.

Second, do you have the technical ability to get your body in the right position to make challenges, without giving away a free kick or—worse still—a penalty? Are you in good enough shape to take on the challenge without running out of steam for the rest of the game? Luckily, you have control over this one.

When you are assigned to man mark an opponent, your goal is to keep your opponent from dominating the game in a way that creates goal-scoring chances. They can still dominate the game in terms of possession and time on the ball, but if you can make sure that the time they spend on the ball is away from your goal, then you have done your job. You can do that by making sure they don't receive the final pass before a goal, and that they don't beat you in critical 1v1 situations.

TRY IT

It's important that you stay close to your opponent, but if you get too close, you can be beaten by a sharp turn or a change of pace. High up the field away from your goalkeeper, you need to make sure that you stay on your goal side of your opponent when they get the ball so that you can see them. You are preventing them from making a pass to their goalkeeper or toward the center line. Better yet, you want to grab that ball and send it to a teammate who can pass the ball closer to your team's goal-scoring range. In the middle third of the field when your opponent has the ball, try to get about an arm and a half's length away from them, to keep them under pressure. In your defending third, close that space down to an arm's length. The key to man marking is to stay focused on *them* when they pass—don't follow the ball. The ball can't score on its own!

COACH'S CORNER TIPS

Keep your focus in the game on the moment you are in. Your ability to pay attention to the right thing at the right time is called attentional control. This is just as important as your technical and tactical ability.

LEVEL 1 **2** 3

Pressing to Get the Ball Back

TYPE OF STRATEGY: Defense attacking in small groups

TEAMS TO WATCH: AC Milan (1987–1991), coach Arrigo Sacchi; Manchester City (2016–2023), coach Pep Guardiola; Borussia Dortmund (2008–2015), coach Jürgen Klopp.

Pressing can be defined as a specific, aggressive (but safe!) defensive play. At times, pressing looks like a pack of wild dogs chasing after the ball, so there has to be some structure and purpose to it. Have I emphasized the importance of communication enough?

We can press for maybe 30 seconds at the most before we run out of steam. That is called the press being broken. It's very rare to see pressing go for very long before some other event kicks into play. Common times to press include an opponent's throw-in, a long ball that is difficult to receive, and a ball that is passed behind the opponent that "leaves them blind" and forces them to turn their back on the play.

We can look for cues that tell us to set up the press in other instances as well. If the opposition's ball carrier has a bad touch on the ball and has to recover, this can give us an opportunity to press for the ball. If the player in possession finds themselves near the out-of-bounds line, we can use the line as another defender and try to either win the ball back or force a throw-in. If it's our throw-in, we have won possession; if it's their throw, we now have time to set up a more structured press. Win-win.

TRY IT

You need a minimum of three players to press effectively. The first defender initializes pressure on the ball carrier. The second defender gets close to cover the first defender, and if possible,

double-teams the ball carrier. The third defender covers the players around the ball. That third player is there to keep pressure on the ball if it gets passed or if the ball carrier escapes. In that case, the third defender needs to get to the ball almost immediately. Supporting defenders must quickly back up that third player.

The first defender's job is not necessarily to win the ball, though if they can nick it away, that's always a bonus. The first defender's job is simply to contain and delay the ball carrier so that the second and third defenders can get to the scene. Before the first player initiates the press, they need to know which supporting players are close by or the press will be broken quickly. Be aware of your surroundings before diving in. As the ball carrier is approached, the first player can slow down to not get beaten easily and focus on containment. They actually want to try to make the opponent keep possession. The second defender needs to approach quickly and from an angle that cuts off an escape. Once the ball carrier is double-teamed, you can challenge for the ball, but don't be overly aggressive, because you don't want to give a foul away. If you get this right, the third defender should take up a covering position that also cuts off any passing lanes and puts them in a position to intercept any pass.

COACH'S CORNER TIPS

Before training or a game, clear your mind of any clutter. This will lower the chances of feeling anxious or worried. These feelings have a negative impact on your performance.

MEET THE SOCCER STAR
KYLIAN MBAPPÉ

Birth Date: December 20, 1998

Position: Forward

Teams: Monaco, Paris Saint-Germain, Real Madrid, and France

Kylian Mbappé was born in Paris and grew up in the northeastern part of the city. Soccer runs through Kylian's family. His father was a soccer coach, his younger brother is a professional soccer player, and his older adopted brother was also a soccer player.

Kylian started his career at Monaco in 2015 when he was sixteen. In August 2017, Kylian moved to Paris Saint-Germain and became the most expensive teenager in world soccer. During his time in Paris, he scored an amazing 162 goals in only 172 games—almost one goal per game. He became the highest goal scorer in Paris Saint-Germain's history.

After six years in Paris, he made his next move to the Spanish team Real Madrid in June of 2024. 80,000 Madrid fans came to the stadium to watch him sign his contract!

At the international level Kylian has won major honors for France. At the 2018 **FIFA (Fédération Internationale de Football Association)** World Cup, he became the youngest French goal scorer in World Cup history.

When Kylian plays, he always creates a problem for the other team. There isn't a defender in the world who can mark him. Kylian has great strength and speed, and he uses these abilities to create many chances. He is also a very good finisher, which is why he has scored almost a goal a game over his career so far. He has mastered the art of dribbling, so he can beat his man not just with speed and strength but also with trickery.

Kylian Mbappé is a superstar, and there is no telling what kind of records he will set throughout his career.

LEVEL

1

2

3

Defending Crosses

TYPE OF STRATEGY: Defense clearing the ball

PLAYER TO WATCH: Virgil van Dijk, player for Groningen, Celtic, Southampton, Liverpool, and the Netherlands

GAME TO WATCH: 2019 Champions League Final, Liverpool vs. Tottenham Hotspur

Although we know that a high percentage of goals comes through the middle field on the top of our 18, we still have to deal with a number of crosses. Very often the middle field is well protected, and our opponents are looking for space in wide positions. Since it's a little simpler to defend the middle field just by adding either a defensive holding midfielder or employing a midfielder to play in front of our **back four**, if you can develop your ability to defend crosses, then you'll become a valuable asset to your team. Your ability to defend crosses may allow your coach to get another player into the central areas when you are defending and allow your team to force the ball wide and away from the danger areas at the top of your 18.

Defending crosses isn't always about heading the ball away, and on the smaller field, the ball isn't in the air as often as on the larger field. You must be prepared to use whatever part of your body is available to block the cross. Remember, it's vital that when you go to block a cross, your hands are away from the ball and, if possible, hidden behind your body.

TRY IT

Your initial focus should always be on the ball carrier and the ball. If you look away at the key moment of delivery, then it doesn't matter how good your marking is, because you will not be able to locate the ball and its trajectory. Take up a position where you can see the ball and be aware of the space that the player on the ball is trying to get the ball into. Try to be aware of what the attacking players are doing. Where are they coming from? Are they coming in on a straight line or making a run on an angle? What speed are they traveling at? Are they looking at the ball like you are, or are they looking at a space that they are trying to get to?

Being aware of what attacking players are doing will give you vital information. If they are looking at the player crossing the ball, then they are also looking for a cue. You can look for that cue, too! If they are not looking at the ball carrier, then they know what is coming and they are trying to get to a certain space. Your job, then, is to stop the ball getting to that space; you will need to take up a position that allows you to do that. The ideal position is in a line between the ball carrier and the area they are trying to hit. If you can get to this position and turn your hips away from your goal, you will limit deflections toward your goal.

You need to be aware of the attacking players around you, but your focus should be on the ball carrier. This way you can get yourself into the right place to either block the cross, intercept the cross and win possession, or beat your opponent in a 1v1 matchup when the ball is crossed. Any of these situations is a win!

COACH'S CORNER TIPS

Self-reflection can help you improve your preparation and performance by thinking about what you did in the game and how you reacted to the things that happened. Three key questions to ask yourself are: What did I do well? What can I do better? What will I do differently next time?

LEVEL ① ② ③

Playing Out of the Back: Defense

TYPE OF STRATEGY: Defense attacking, build up play, passing

TEAMS TO WATCH: Spanish National Team (2008–2012), Barcelona (2008–2012), Manchester City (2023), Arsenal (early 2000s to 2006)

When your team has a goal kick, you have two options: Your keeper or a central defender can kick it away from your goal into, at best, a 50–50 situation for you. Or you can try to pass the ball from the goal kick to one of your teammates, keep possession, and play from the back through midfield and into your opponent's half. At some stages of a game, that big kick downfield may be the answer, but most of the time trying to keep the ball and build play through your team is the best option.

Of course, trying to play from the back has its risks. The ball is closer to your goal, and if you make a mistake and lose possession, then it might be easier for your opponent to score.

There are a few reasons why playing out of the back is a good idea. First, it's hard to score when you don't have the ball. If your team has possession, then unless you score an own goal (where you accidentally score in your own net), your opponent cannot score. If they cannot score, your team cannot be defeated. It's more fun to have the ball than it is to chase the ball!

TRY IT

If you are comfortable in possession and confident in your ability to receive the ball, then you will succeed in this style of play. The keys to playing out of the back include: 1) movement into space to create room to receive the ball, 2) the timing of that movement, 3) your first touch on the ball, 4) knowing where your teammates and opponents are, and 5) getting fully or half

turned with your hips to the sideline when you receive the ball. You may wonder in panic: *Is that all?* Relax. You can control all of those key factors.

If you make your move too early, you become easy to mark and take yourself out of the play. It's much better to move away from the ball and open up some space to go back into, in order to receive the ball. As the ball is coming to you, it's important to get your body in a position where you can see what is happening behind you, so you have all the information needed to make the best decision. Remember, if you don't like the pass or situation you find yourself in, you can always go back to the keeper, who has the option to then clear the ball. Have confidence and believe in your ability to receive the ball close to the goal with pressure. The other team will sense any hesitation and jump. Once you learn your part in playing out of the back, you become a key member of the team.

COACH'S CORNER TIPS

When you reflect on your game, think about how well you did to prepare before the game, both mentally and physically. Were you ready to go? How did you start the game? Did you want to get the ball or were you away from the action?

LEVEL

Crossing the Ball to the Danger Zone

TYPES OF STRATEGIES: Offense attacking, ball striking

PLAYER TO WATCH: Trent Alexander-Arnold, player for Liverpool, Real Madrid, and England

GAME TO WATCH: 2021 Liverpool vs. Arsenal

FIFA reports that the majority of goals in their major tournaments are scored through the central area on top of the 18-yard box, sometimes called zone 14. Since zone 14 is so well-known by coaches, many teams make sure that they protect this space closely. In order to do this, they try to force the team into wide areas. Being able to make dangerous crosses from wide positions adds a valuable attacking option for your team.

Crossing the ball is about making good contact with it and getting it into areas where your teammates can attack and even have goal potential. Part of crossing the ball is certainly about decision-making: Should you cross the ball or keep moving toward the goal? Should you cross the ball or pass the ball back, so your team has a better scoring opportunity? These are questions that you will learn to answer over time. If you become consistent with your delivery, these questions will answer themselves. Your teammates will learn to make runs into dangerous positions, because they know that you can deliver on demand.

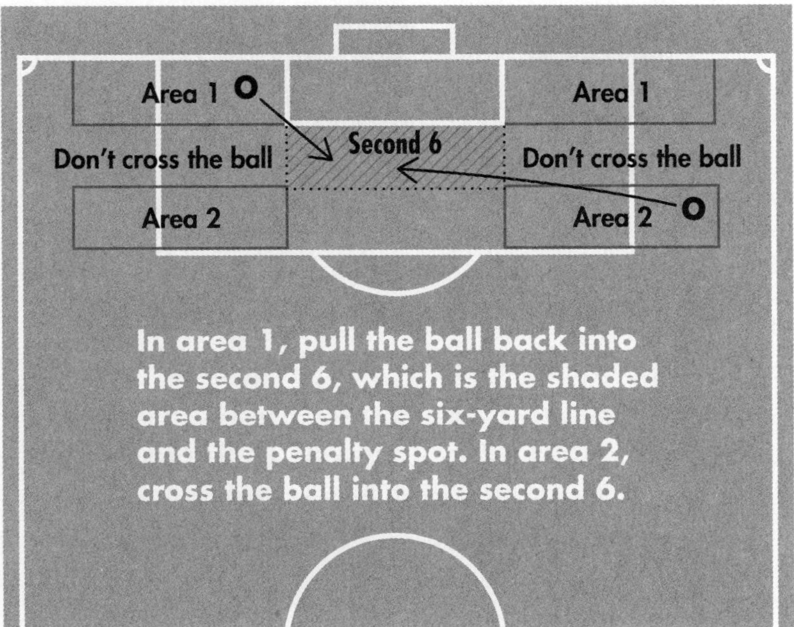

TRY IT

The first thing to think about is location. Into what areas do you want to deliver the ball? Occasionally you may "pick a player out" with a cross. But, perhaps surprisingly, in most cases you are trying to hit into open space, with the aim of your teammate getting to the ball first. You pick a space where you feel confident your attacker can be successful.

Try to hit the space that we call the **second six**. This area is a little too far for the keeper to come for the ball with certainty, but it's just the right space for your teammates to have a chance to one touch the ball into the goal with either their forehead or foot. If the ball goes into the second six at a slow or medium pace, it allows the defenders a little more time to react and clear.

If the ball is driven in at pace, it favors your players. It can cause mayhem when it comes to deflections, so I would encourage you to keep your eye on the ball and deliver the ball with some hot sauce on it! Whether you send the ball in the air or on the ground is very much situational. Select the right technique and deliver a killer cross. The benefit to keeping the ball on the ground is that most soccer players are better with their feet than their head. A good cross will set up a good goal-scoring chance.

COACH'S CORNER TIPS

After a game, take some time to reflect on how the game went. How did you play? What was your best moment of the game? What are some areas you can do better? How did you react to any feedback from your coach? Ask your IST to help you with these questions.

Finishing Crosses: Scoring off a Pass

TYPE OF STRATEGY: Offense attacking

PLAYER TO WATCH: Erling Haaland, player for Bryne, Molde, Red Bull Salzburg, Borussia Dortmund, Manchester City, and Norway

GAME TO WATCH: 2024–2025 Champions League, Manchester City vs. Sparta Prague

PLAYER TO WATCH: Ruud van Nistelrooy, player for Den Bosch, Heerenveen, PSV Eindhoven, Manchester United, Real Madrid, Hamburger SV, Málaga, and the Netherlands

GAMES TO WATCH: Manchester United vs. Everton (2003–2004)

There isn't a better scene in the game than a cross going into the 18-yard penalty box and a player making a perfectly timed run to score a goal. These goals are part of the folklore of every club in the world. Finishing crosses is a learned skill. Like anything that we learn, we need to accept that we will have some misses along the way. But what exactly does finishing crosses mean?

Every offensive player's dream is to get to the ball and put it in the goal. You can only control what you do, and, in this case, you need to focus on the process of hitting the target. The ball only has to cross the line for a goal. If you start to focus on the scoring part of the equation, then you are not fully in control; the other team has a goalkeeper whose only job is to stop the ball going into the goal. You can't control what they do. In my experience, when players start to think about scoring the goal, they also start to think about how they will celebrate. Before they know it, the ball has either gone past them, or they have smashed it too far into orbit!

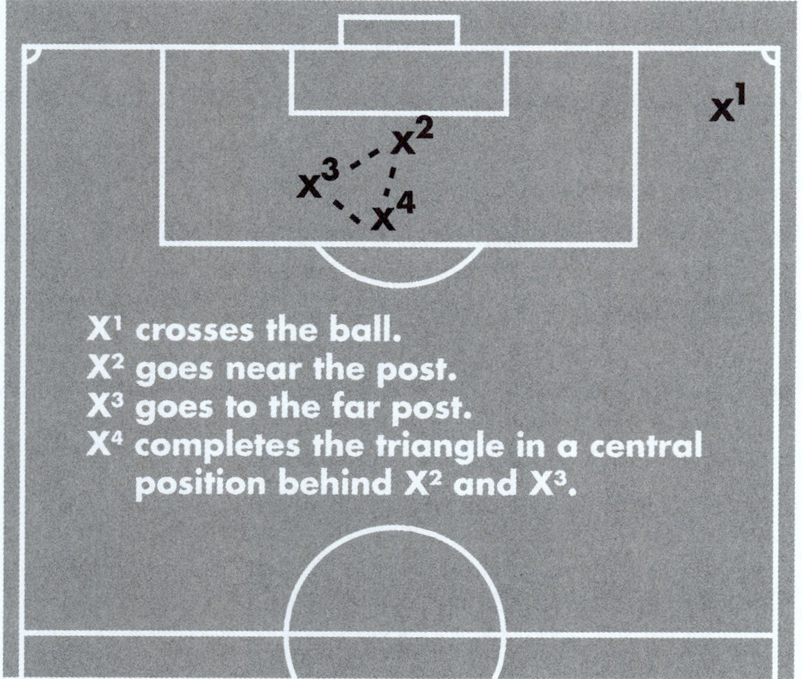

TRY IT

Timing and technique are the two things that will help you put the ball on target. If both of these are working well, there is a good chance you will have enough power and accuracy on the ball to take it past the keeper. But even the most miraculous run and dive to the ball counts for nothing if it goes wide or over the bar. The other team then ends up with the advantage of a goal kick.

There are three areas that you should focus on when the ball is crossed: the near post area, the far post area, and the central area in front of the goal between six and eighteen yards out. Each area has a different approach.

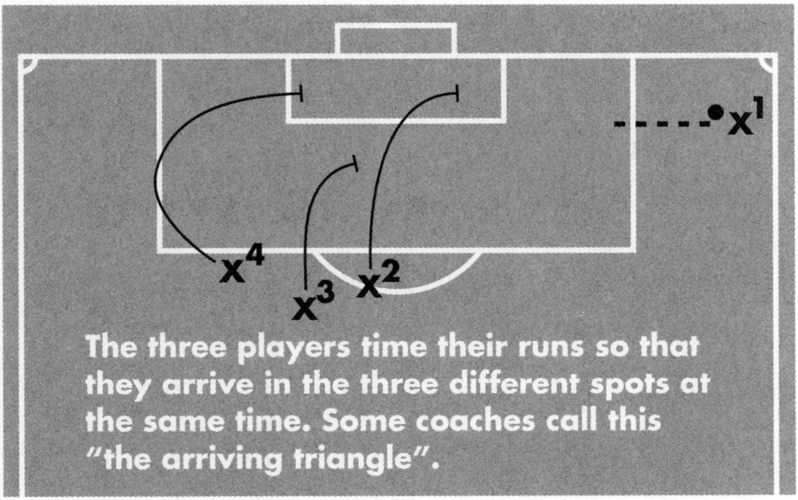

The three players time their runs so that they arrive in the three different spots at the same time. Some coaches call this "the arriving triangle".

If you are attacking the near post area, you are trying to get across the defenders. If you make contact with the ball before it crosses the near post, then you are helping the ball on its way by trying to change the angle of the ball with one touch. In the far post area, you are looking for an area to position yourself in hopes that everyone else misses the ball and it comes to you. In this far post area, you will have more time than you think, so you might be able to take a touch before you hit the target. In the central area, you are reacting to the ball and the space you are in. Focus on your balance and getting good contact on the ball toward the goal.

Get into the right position to put the ball on net and make the keeper make a save. If they fail, it's a goal!

COACH'S CORNER TIPS

Stay in control of your emotions, your thoughts, and your behaviors when you feel stress or anxiety. Breathe slowly and deeply, regain your focus, and move on to the next thing.

LEVEL ① ② ❸

Losing Opponents in Their 18

TYPES OF STRATEGIES: Offense attacking, movement on and off the ball

PLAYER TO WATCH: Gabriel Jesus, player for Palmeiras, Manchester City, Arsenal, and Brazil

GAME TO WATCH: 2024 Carabao Cup, Arsenal vs. Crystal Palace

The space in your opponent's penalty area is precious to both teams. This is your chance to score, which is the last thing they want to happen. There is hardly any space behind their defensive line. If you go looking for space away from the goal, then you are making your job harder. Yes, movement away from the goal may take a defender with you to create space for a teammate, but here we are talking about losing your opponent in their penalty area so that you are open when the ball comes to you. One of the most frustrating things in the game is when you lose your opponent, find yourself unmarked, and don't receive the ball. Be prepared to do the work to get away from your opponent and get open, especially in the 18, where space is hard to find.

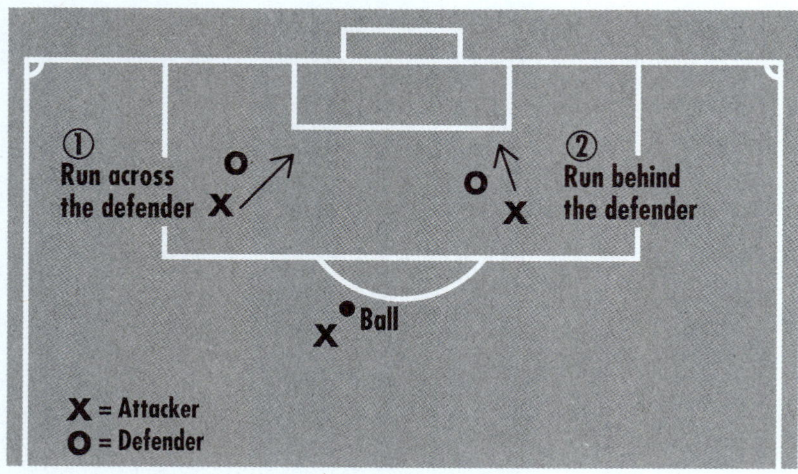

TRY IT

So how do you do this? I would advise you to go where you *want* the ball to be. If you consistently get into open spaces in goal-scoring areas, then in time you will score goals. When the ball is high up the field and you are in the opponent's penalty area, it's safe to say that your opponents will be thinking about the ball, trying to cover the dangerous space, and also trying to find you. Force them to find you before they look back to check on the ball.

The type and timing of your movements are vital, and there are three options.

1. If you make a move across the face of the defender, they will see you and lock on. You need to be across from them at pace. This may mean you will only get one free touch before the defender gets near enough to close you down.

2. A better movement would be behind the shoulder of your opponent; the defender will follow the ball, but you will have more time when you receive it.

3. The best move is one where you lose the defender because of your movement, a combination of 1 and 2. Make your first move either across or behind your opponent as they pick up this move, then change direction and explode into the space that they have just left. This gives you the separation you need, and the defender will not be able to recover in time.

COACH'S CORNER TIPS

Stay committed to the process. Learn, practice, and see it through to the end, even when you are challenged. It's the hard things we do that make the difference to our performance.

MEET THE SOCCER STAR
ABBY WAMBACH

Birth Date: June 2, 1980

Position: Forward

Teams: Washington Freedom, Ajax, magicJack, Western New York Flash, and the United States

Abby Wambach was born in Rochester, New York. During her high school career, she scored 142 goals and was named to the High School All-America team in her senior season. She was considered the top college recruit, and in her freshman year at college, she led the Florida Gators to their first NCAA title in women's soccer. She was a great goal scorer and scored 96 goals for the Gators in her four-year career.

Abby went on to play for the U.S. Women's National Team. She played in four World Cups, and she is a two-time Olympic medalist, winning gold in 2004 and 2012. In total, Abby scored 184 goals for the U.S. Women's team in a career that lasted 255 games.

Abby was the youngest child in her family, growing up with two older sisters and four older brothers. From an early age she had to learn how to compete and also how to win, lose, and be humble. Her older siblings never let her win; she had to earn it. This rough-and-tumble childhood helped her playing ability, as it made her a strong physical player. She also had great strength inside. Just before the 2008 Olympics, Abby broke her left leg. This was a huge disappointment for her. However, her inner strength and will to play helped her recovery, and thirteen months later she was back scoring goals for the U.S. Women's National Team.

Abby Wambach was a trailblazer in women's soccer and set high standards for today's players to follow.

LEVEL ① ② ❸

Playing with Your Back to the Goal as a Target

TYPES OF STRATEGIES: Offense attacking, touch on the ball, spatial awareness

PLAYER TO WATCH: Olivier Giroud, player for Grenoble, Tours, Montpellier, Arsenal, Chelsea, AC Milan, Los Angeles FC, Lille, and France

GAMES TO WATCH: 2018 World Cup games featuring France

When we win possession, our focus should first be on securing possession, and then on looking to go forward with the ball. If we can't move the ball forward ourselves, then we need to look toward the goal. This pass can go into space (as it often does), or we can play the ball into a player positioned higher up the field. In soccer, we generally call them a "target player," but some coaches may call them a platform player or an advanced player. There is no right or wrong name; the role is the same.

If your team has a strong target player, use them to help you break forward from the back. You also use a target player in counter-attacking situations. In this situation, if you are going to commit players forward, it is vital that the target player is able to play with their back to the goal and hold off the defender. Very often the target player is isolated, so they must have a good first touch and be smart enough and strong enough to hold off one (or sometimes two) defenders, to give your supporting players time to get close to them. The target player needs to hold and control the ball long enough for supporting players to get in position to receive the next pass. However, if your target player is isolated in a 1v1 situation, they can try to turn the defender and go to goal.

TRY IT

When playing this role, the first thing you have to do is stay as high up the field as possible, in order to stretch the opposition and open up spaces for your supporting players to exploit. You have to fight the urge to drop back and help get the ball, because your role is to be available when your team does win it back. As they do, you should be moving to a space where you can secure the ball and keep possession. Try to get to an area that gives you some opportunities to escape pressure; sidelines might not be a great spot, because you will run out of space.

As the ball is coming to you, make sure to look over your shoulder to see where the pressure will be coming from. Ideally, you want your first touch to be with your feet. If the ball is coming to you in the air, try to get it to the ground as soon as possible. When the ball is on the ground and under control, position it as far away from the pressuring defender as you can while still keeping contact with it. If you position yourself with your hips facing the sideline, that will help keep your whole body between the defender and the ball. Get your head up and look for a teammate to link up with, but also be aware of opportunities to turn and roll the defender if they get too close to you. If you can beat the defender, it may set you up for a 1v1 against the keeper—a great place to be!

COACH'S CORNER TIPS

View challenges as opportunities for growth and learning instead of seeing them as a threat. Challenges are meant to be overcome. Don't be afraid to step outside of your comfort zone.

LEVEL

Creating Space on the Field

TYPES OF STRATEGIES: Team formation, attacking, movement with and without the ball

PLAYER TO WATCH: Lamine Yamal, player for Barcelona and Spain

GAME TO WATCH: 2024–25 Champions League, Barcelona vs. Benfica

The questions we should always be asking ourselves in the game are: 1) Where is space available on the field, 2) How can I use that space to my advantage, 3) Can I create more space with my movement, and 4) Where is the most dangerous space I can occupy? Space is very often found in wide positions. Why? Teams will protect the center of the field, because that is where most goals come from. If you find some free space, sometimes just staying there will create an opening for a teammate, because you will attract attention from defenders. If you move the defenders, then there is a space you can fill. When trying to create space, you will be more effective if you can engage the opponent, move them around, and disrupt their defensive shape.

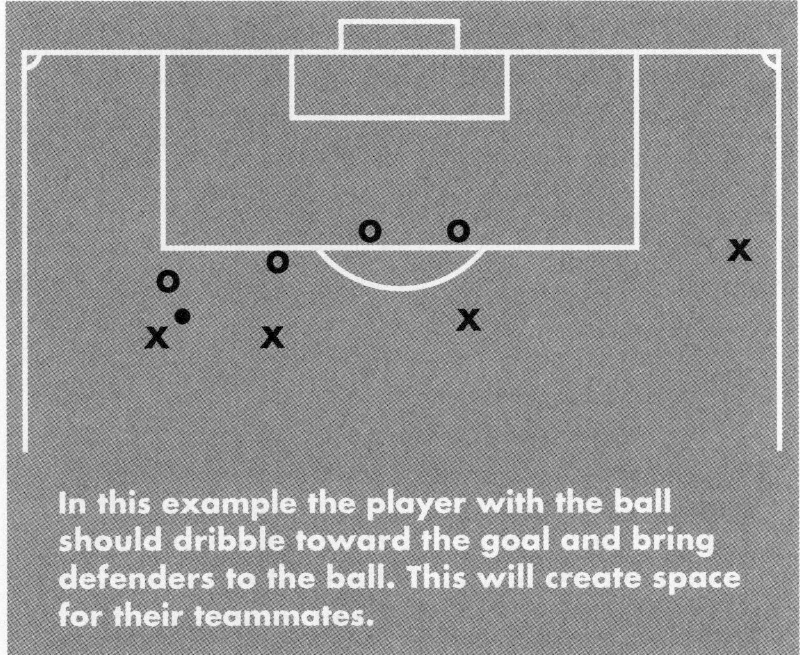

In this example the player with the ball should dribble toward the goal and bring defenders to the ball. This will create space for their teammates.

TRY IT

When you are trying to create space, the first thing to think about is movement. In order to create space, you need to get into a position where your movement will attract attention from defenders and disrupt your opponent. It's tough to create space when you are in space; if the defender can get in a position where they can see you and the ball and the space that you want to move to, then they can deal with you quite easily. It's a different story if you can get into a position where you can create space in unpredictable ways. The best example I can think of is getting about two to three yards away from the defender, but in a position in line with their shoulders.

From this position, you can do three different things that will create space for you *and* your teammates:

1. You can make a run in behind the defender, either in a straight line or in a diagonal line. This puts you into space where you can receive the ball or take the defender with you and open up the space you just left.

2. You can make a run across the front of the defender in a horizontal line or a diagonal line. This will attract the attention of the defender. They will most likely follow you inside and leave an open space for someone to fill.

3. You can drop back a little, either to receive the ball and take on the defender, or to receive the ball and attract the defender to the ball. The best thing about this strategy is that you don't have to receive the ball to create space, because you have successfully moved the defender.

COACH'S CORNER TIPS

Reflect on how you managed your emotions in a game. Ask yourself: How did I respond to things that didn't go my way? What goals did I set in the game, and were they realistic? How did I react to any success in the game and how did that feel? These questions will help you work on the mental side of the game and play a part in your goal-setting process.

Keeping the Ball Safe When Passing or in Possession

TYPES OF STRATEGIES: Attacking, build up play

PLAYER TO WATCH: Toni Kroos, player Bayer Leverkusen, Bayern Munich, Real Madrid, and Germany

GAME TO WATCH: 2014 Champions League, Bayern Munich vs. Arsenal

---

What does keeping the ball safe mean to you? If you asked me that question I would probably answer something like this: *When I have the ball, I want to keep it in a place where my opponent can't get to it unless they foul me. In that case, we'd get a free kick and we'd get the ball back. When I am passing the ball, I want to make sure that I pass it to a space that allows my teammate to get the ball and keep it safe as easily as possible.*

In this section I will cover ball security and give you a couple of different scenarios. I am going to talk mostly about keeping the ball safe when we pass it. Your direction of pass can make a big difference here. If you pass forward, then the defenders will be a little closer to your teammate. If you pass across the field, your teammate might not be covered so closely, so this may be a simpler option. Finally, if you pass back toward your own goal, there is a possibility that will be a safer pass, as you are doing the other team's job for them, going away from their goal, and they may let you do that.

Let's think about a forward pass, because if you can do that well, the other passes will take care of themselves. The first thing to think about is where the safe space is. This is a space on the field where the ball is closer to your teammate than their opponent. For example, if you are in a central position and you are playing a forward pass to the right side of the field, then it's likely that the defender would be in front of your teammate. If you make a pass just behind your teammate, then you are making a pass to what we call the "safe side." If you pass it out in front of them, then there is a chance that when it gets to space, the defender may be closer to the ball than your teammate and that's not good. You can always play the ball just behind your teammate, no more than three feet, and they will more than likely retain the ball. That's a safe pass!

The next thing to think about is if you can help your teammate beat their opponent when they get the ball. In this pass, again to the right, take a look at the space in front of your teammate and behind the defender. If there is space, you play a safe pass into this area and take a little risk. The key here is that, if the defender is in the right place, they will be inside of your teammate, closer to the center of the field. If this is the case, then you can play a longer pass behind the defender, but you have to put more weight on the pass since you want it to go closer to the sideline. This gives your teammate a good chance to get there first because they don't have to turn and can run in a straight line. See Mid-Range Passing (page 44) and Bending the Ball: Inside of Foot (page 50).

Be patient as you master this in practice and use it in the games. Remember: The higher up the field you are, the more risk you can take!

COACH'S CORNER TIPS

Remember when packing your equipment bag to add a snack that you eat an hour before the game and make sure you have enough fluids. If you feel thirsty, you're already dehydrated!

PART 4

Preparing for the Move to Full Field

In this section I will talk about what happens when you move to the full-field 11-a-side game. This will happen at around the U13 age level, but some areas may introduce this a little earlier. You may have already made this move, and in that case this information will help you now. If not, this is a chance to get a head start on your teammates and opponents by looking into the future.

I want to encourage you to watch as much soccer as you can, preferably in person so that you can see the whole field and watch how the players work together. On TV, you can watch the UEFA Champions League, MLS, and NWSL, as there are lots of different formations. For each formation covered, I will explain where each group of players fits in—defenders, midfielders, and attackers—and will talk about some of the different roles of the formation. Finally, I'll give examples of how and why a formation can help a team in the game and what problems may occur.

Before we start, it's really important to let you know that no formation ever won a game. The formation doesn't score goals, and it doesn't let them in, either. That's the role of the player!

LEVEL

1 2 3

4-4-2

TYPE OF STRATEGY: Team formation

TEAM TO WATCH: Italy, games from the 2006 FIFA World Cup

Four defenders, four midfielders, and two strikers (also known as forwards) is quite possibly the most common formation used in soccer. This doesn't mean it's the easiest or simplest way to line up. Many coaches will use this formation as a backup strategy if the original plan isn't working, so it's important that you have a good understanding of it.

TRY IT

Knowing where your position needs to be and where the ball is are the two most important things in this formation. The movement of the group almost adds another player to the team. Whenever you are watching a game on TV and you get a wide angle shot of the field, hit pause and take a look at the shape of the teams in relation to the ball. Once you have an understanding of this playing system, it will be imprinted on your brain! Believe me when I tell you that it's like riding a bike—once you have it, it never leaves you.

WHY IT WORKS

In my opinion, 4-4-2 is the easiest system to teach. It is well structured and defensively solid. The back four have a pattern and, in general, the midfield four will mimic that pattern in front of the back line. This means that once a team understands the shape of the formation, it's very easy to slip into.

Wide midfielders play in front of and help cover the full-backs, central midfielders help cover the central defenders, and

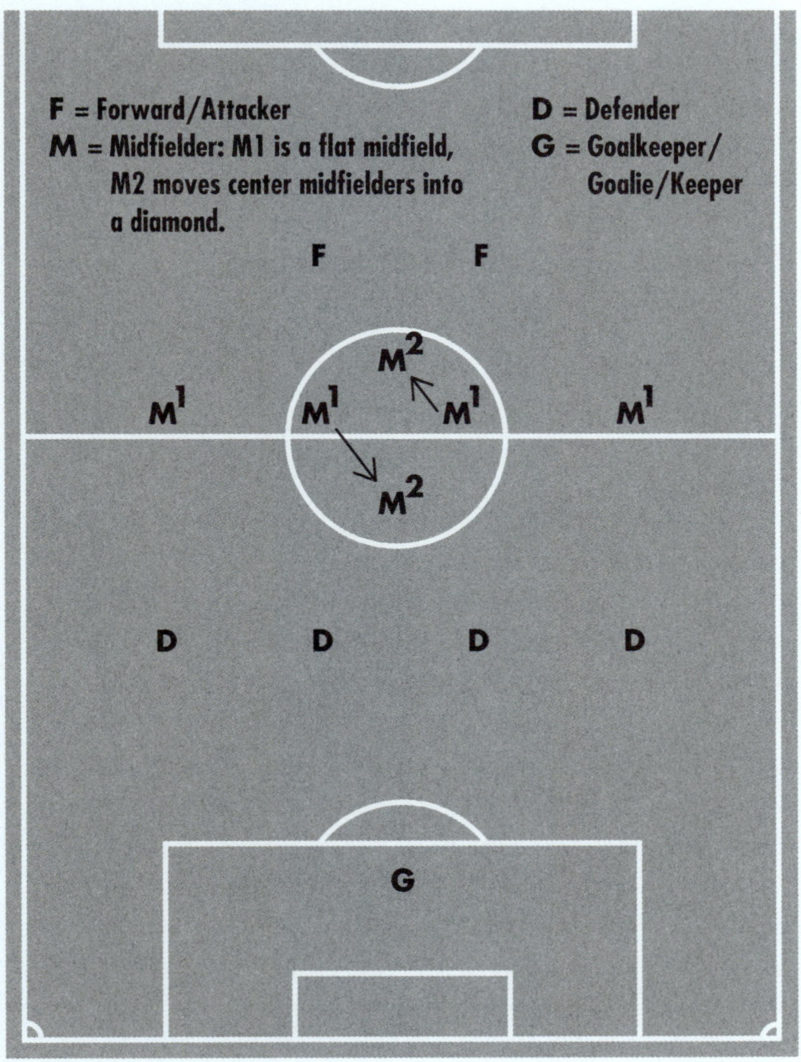

when the fullbacks overlap, the wide midfielder knows they have to hold and cover.

It also allows fullbacks to get forward and have a high starting position that's closer to where your team can score. If you are playing as a fullback and can get up toward the halfway line in possession, you become a threat to opponents.

This system also encourages wing play, since the two outside midfielders take on the role of wingers when in possession. If they get enough of the ball, they can create a lot of chances for their team.

WHERE THERE CAN BE PROBLEMS

The structure of 4-4-2 can also be one of its weaknesses. It is easy for opponents to drift in between the line and pull players out of position when playing against 4-4-2. Once a defensive player is pulled out of position, gaps and holes are created for opponents to fill.

When defending deep in your half, it is important that the two central defenders mark up on players. If one of them takes a free covering role (covering whoever is near them instead of picking a specific person), then the fullback on the opposite side of the field will get pulled into the center of the field. This then means that the wide midfielder has to drop back and cover the fullback spot. That leaves five players in the back and limits your opportunity to break out with numbers; you have one less player in the midfield and one less player to support the forwards.

Defensively, the midfield four must become more compact. Very often the wide midfielder stays too wide and is unable to help win the ball back, and is also too far away to reach with a transition pass when you win possession.

COACH'S CORNER TIPS

Work on building your confidence. You have to believe in your ability and stay positive even when things are tough. Trust yourself to get the job done, and if it doesn't work out, get ready for the next one.

LEVEL ① ❷ ③

4-3-3

TYPE OF STRATEGY: Team formation

TEAMS TO WATCH: Real Madrid (2022–2025), Manchester City (2022–2025), Bayern Munich (2022–2025)

This formation of play gives the team four defenders, three midfielders, and three strikers left on offense. It relies on the players being connected and moving into different positions at different times in the game.

TRY IT

Playing with four defenders, three midfielders, and three strikers gives a team a little more flexibility throughout a game, since this formation is the most interchangeable. From 4-3-3 you can easily move to 4-4-2 or 3-4-3 if required, by simply moving a wide striker back to a wide midfield position or moving a wide defender into a wide midfield position. Players can stay the same and the structural change is very simple. At times this formation can be very fluid, with defenders stepping into midfield, strikers dropping back into midfield, and midfielders taking up advanced positions and making supporting runs. You have to be flexible enough to play across all three lines in this system and take on the responsibilities of different roles at different times.

WHY IT WORKS

Maybe the greatest strength in this formation is offense. Playing with three strikers gives you width high up the field and allows you to isolate the opponent's defenders in 1v1 situations. In addition, 4-3-3 allows you to get your fullbacks higher up the field, because the midfield three will play more centrally to create space in wide areas for your fullbacks to fill.

F = Forward/Attacker

M = Midfielder

D = Defender

G = Goalkeeper/Goalie/Keeper

F

F F

M M

M

D D

D D

G

When your team has the ball and can get the fullbacks forward, it almost becomes like playing with four midfielders and three strikers. This means you can have seven players in advancing positions, which allows you to overpower your opponent in their half. This is something that you should look to do as often as possible.

Playing with three strikers also means that very often your opponent won't push their fullback forward, because leaving them man-to-man at the back is in your favor. Surprisingly, you can also outnumber your opponents in the center of the field if they play 4-4-2, as your three midfielders can start in narrower positions.

WHERE THERE CAN BE PROBLEMS

Having three strikers up front is good, but that can also be a problem when you don't have the ball. One of the strikers must come back into midfield in order to help your team regain possession or delay the opponent's attack. This sounds pretty straightforward, but not all strikers like to come back and defend! If the three of them stay up top all the time, you could get overrun if your opponent gets their fullback forward.

The midfield three can also be exposed if your opponent can switch the play quickly, because three people will always find it harder to cover the width of the field than four. The midfield players also need to make sure that they don't get caught square, playing in a straight line; one pass will beat all three of them. Three players in midfield can leave the center backs a little exposed, because there is usually only one of the midfielders playing in a screening role in front of them.

The midfielders must be dynamic in their movement and have a good understanding of the signals and cues of the opponent. At the same time, wide defenders will have to step into the midfield to stop the team getting outmaneuvered in the middle of the field.

COACH'S CORNER TIPS

Overtraining can lead to mental fatigue, burnout, and a lack of motivation. Make sure you find time to rest and do other activities. Overtraining can also lead to overuse injuries, which are hard to rehab. Make sure you are never more than three days from a rest period.

3-4-3

TYPE OF STRATEGY: Team formation

TEAMS TO WATCH: Chelsea (2017), coach Antonio Conte; Chelsea (2021), coach Thomas Tuchel

LEVEL ① ② ❸

This formation has three defenders, who very often play centrally and cover the width of the penalty area. There are four midfielders who can play either flat, in a straight line, or in a diamond formation with one of the central midfielders playing in an advance position and the other one playing just behind them. Finally, there are three strikers, with the central striker playing farther forward than the other two strikers who will play as wingers.

TRY IT

If you play in a 3-4-3 role it's really important that you are paying attention all the time as this formation is very fluid. The two wide midfielders can help defensively when your team doesn't have the ball by dropping back to help cover the back three and almost becoming a back four. If your opponent has the ball in a wide position and if the ball is central then it almost becomes a back five. This means that if you are playing in one of those positions you must be alert. The two central midfielders also need to stay focused to stop attacks through the middle of the field and be ready to support the three strikers, particularly in the center of the field.

The front three players can stay a little higher up the field when your team is defending. That helps in two ways: the opponent can't keep sending players forward as they have to mark your attackers, and when your team gets the ball, you have some options to pass forward.

Watch teams that play this formation and think about the roles of the players and where you think you are the best fit.

WHY IT WORKS

This formation has great flexibility and offers a lot of balance across the field. It also helps you dominate the middle of the field, particularly when you are playing in a diamond formation. When the other team has the ball, you can have five players focused on defending—the back three combined with the two central players or the two wide players depending on how your team defends.

When you have the ball, you have at least five players committed to the attack, either through the center or in wide areas of the field. The flexibility of this formation allows your team to outnumber your opponent at different times in wide areas. When you have possession you can also fill the midfield and keep the ball as you have more players in that space.

WHERE THERE CAN BE PROBLEMS

There are three areas where this formation can be put under pressure. If the wide midfielders are out of position, then the wide spaces that would normally be covered by fullbacks in a back four are wide open. This means the back three will be stretched and pulled out of position, possibly even into 1v1 situations that you want to avoid.

If you are playing a team that has three midfielders, then your two central midfielders are outnumbered. This threatens your back three and again exposes them to 1v1 situations.

The last problem is in the midfield. If your team plays in a diamond formation, then you risk creating a hole in the middle of the field inside your lines. See Breaking Lines and Living in the Triangle (page 74). If your opponent can get a player into that space and play between your lines, then they can break your defensive lines with well-timed passes to wide players who can then attack your back three. If your midfield four plays flatter, then you are always under threat of one well-timed pass taking all four players out of the game and exposing your back three.

COACH'S CORNER TIPS

Team sports create a competitive environment, which can lead to conflict. Don't seek conflict; learn to manage it and you will become a more resilient person and athlete.

LEVEL ① ② ❸

3-5-2

TYPE OF STRATEGY: Team formation

TEAM TO WATCH: Inter Milan (2023)

Playing with three defenders can be a risk. But if you play with three in the back, then that means you can have an extra player somewhere else on the field. As you know, soccer is sometimes like chess. A big question in soccer is "How do we get an extra player on the field without adding an extra player on the field?"

TRY IT

When you are playing in this formation, it's critical that you fully understand your role, particularly if you fill one of the five positions in midfield. Make sure to understand not just your job, but also the jobs of your teammates. If you aren't clear on these roles, talk with your coach.

If you are playing in a wide position in midfield, your job is to protect the wide spaces behind you as well as the space in front of the three defenders. Make sure you are always aware of the position of the defender behind you. The three central midfielders offer support to the strikers, cover for the three defenders, and aim to win the ball back. It's vital that each player is able to do all three of these things at different times in the game. At times it can feel like the five midfielders are being outplayed; this is usually due to a lack of understanding of individual roles and a lack of leadership within the midfield players. You can be the leader and organizer in the group. Can you become that "extra player" everyone is looking for?

Of all the formations that are mentioned in this book, 3-5-2 is reliant on your understanding of spaces on the field and between players. If you are playing in the back three and get

too close together, then you will leave too much space exposed for your opponent. If you get too spread out, then the spaces in between you will be too big to defend. In midfield, if the five players get too close together, you'll be crowded together and you'll most likely be wasting a player. At the same time, if all five players get too spread out across the field, then you will expose the three defenders to possible threats.

Try to watch teams that play with five midfielders and look at the spaces they fill and how they move together as a group. This will help you understand how to play in this formation.

WHY IT WORKS

Playing with three in the back and five in midfield allows you to outnumber your opponents in the middle of the field, usually 5v4 or sometimes 5v3. This means you can dominate that space and keep possession of the ball. Playing with five in midfield also gives your team the chance to use the full width of the field when in possession of the ball. If you can move the ball quickly enough, your team can create many 1v1 opportunities in wide areas of the field.

Defensively, you can attempt to win the ball higher up the field by flooding the areas in the midfield with your five players. You can also move players around in order to disrupt your opponent. If they want to play out of the back, then you can easily defend from the front by pushing the wide midfielders up to join the two strikers, to create a group of four players who will have a better chance of winning the ball back.

WHERE THERE CAN BE PROBLEMS

Here's the thing: Playing with three in the back can be a risk. If your opponents play with three strikers, you have to go man-to-man across the back line or ask your two wide players to play a little more defensively to cover the back three. This means that you are sacrificing one of the advantages that you hope to gain by playing with three in the back. Changing your plan to adapt to the opponent isn't a great way to start a game.

Sometimes when playing with five in midfield, there can be some confusion. The roles of the wider players are easy to understand, but who is doing what in the center of midfield? Who is the holding midfielder, who is the attacking player, and who is marking whom? Confusion can lead to a lot of problems—and negate the extra player in the center of the field.

COACH'S CORNER TIPS

Show a positive attitude at all times with your body language. Keep your head up and shoulders back and you will be seen as a positive force on your team.

4-2-3-1

TYPE OF STRATEGY: Team formation

TEAM TO WATCH: England Men's team (2012, 2024), coach Gareth Southgate

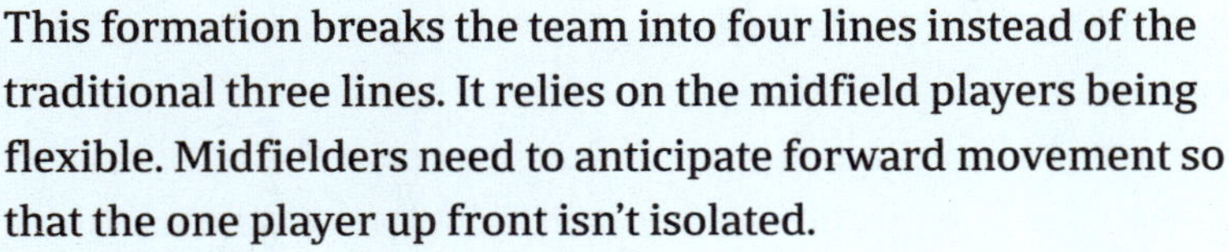

This formation breaks the team into four lines instead of the traditional three lines. It relies on the midfield players being flexible. Midfielders need to anticipate forward movement so that the one player up front isn't isolated.

TRY IT

This system of play is a little different from the other ones in this book, since the team is separated into four groups instead of three. The midfield group is split into two defensive midfielders that protect the back four, and three attacking midfielders who support the single striker. This system can also be called 4-5-1 depending on the mindset of the coach. I think that 4-5-1 is a little more defensive-minded than 4-2-3-1, because you are committing three midfielders to advanced positions.

When you are playing in this system, it's important not to overthink your role. Even though the midfield group is split into defensive midfielders and attacking midfielders, if you occupy one of these roles, your job is that of a midfielder. It's important to understand that at times you may have to cover one of the other roles. This system of play offers a little more flexibility in midfield, but only if the midfielders work together.

WHY IT WORKS

Very often the five midfield players can act as a group and swarm around the opponents when they have the ball. With four players behind them after winning the ball, it is a lot easier to keep possession by playing back to a defender. This system of play can allow you to outnumber your opponent in your defending third and the middle third, so your team can have plenty of possessions.

The two holding defensive midfielders can act as cover for the fullbacks. This system of play really allows the fullbacks to get high up the field and create some 2v2 situations with the wide attacking midfielders in the opponent's half. If your team does a good job of switching play, then you can also get some 2v1 situations, which are great advantages.

This system also allows for supporting runs to the striker from more areas of the field, since the three attacking midfielders will look to "join up" with the striker. You may also get a late run from one of the defensive midfielders or an attacking fullback. Late runs are always the hardest to defend against and lead to many goals.

WHERE THERE CAN BE PROBLEMS

The biggest issue with this system is that you only have one dedicated striker. We see with professional players how hard it is for an isolated striker to have success, so let's be straight here: In the youth game where you are still developing, it will be a big challenge. Another problem with having a single striker is that the opponent can send players forward from the back, as they only have one player to mark. This can make the midfield overcrowded, which can stop creativity because there is less time and space.

The other challenge is that there is often a big, unprotected space in front of your fullback and your wide attacking midfielder. I have seen a lot of youth games where this space was left exposed and the opponent just put a player in that area. That unfairly exposes your fullback. It pulls the defensive midfielder out of position to help the fullback and leaves the middle of the field a little too open. You can't be in two places at once, and you only have ten outfield players, so it's a balancing act to manage placement.

COACH'S CORNER TIPS

When you set your goals, use these three points: 1) think honestly about what you do well and where you need help, 2) evaluate your performance without thinking about the result of the game, 3) and think about what success and failure mean to you. Your IST can support you with this.

LEVEL

4-3-2-1

TYPE OF STRATEGY: Team formation

TEAMS TO WATCH: AC Milan (2003–2007), coach Carlo Ancelotti; England (1996 Euro, England vs. Netherlands), coach Terry Venables

Just like with the 4-2-3-1 system, here we are breaking the team into four units: a defensive line of four, three defensive midfielders, two attacking midfielders, and a single striker. Sometimes we call this formation the Christmas Tree or Pyramid because it has a wide base leading to a narrow point.

This formation is more solid in defense and protects the fullbacks. It also allows them to get into forward positions. When playing this formation as a fullback you will have a lot of opportunities to get forward to support in the attack. If you are a defensive midfielder, then your role is to build a screen in front of the back four, cover the fullbacks when they go forward, and when possible, get a little closer to the attacking group when your team has the ball.

TRY IT

As with 4-2-3-1, the 4-3-2-1 formation could also be called 4-5-1. The difference is the midfield arrangement, with three midfielders playing in front of the back four and two attacking midfielders supporting the striker. It's not a huge change, but it does have some differences.

WHY IT WORKS

This formation is very strong defensively. If your team doesn't score a lot of goals, which can be a common problem, your coach may decide to use this formation in order to protect your goal. Playing in this formation is good for counter-attacking opportunities. The striker needs to stay in a high position to be a target, and then the two attacking midfielders need to quickly support the striker. Because you could have as many as seven players in defensive positions, you will often win the ball back. Your opponent will give you the ball back by taking risks. This will play right in to the hands of counter-attacking teams.

The five midfielders can overpower the opponent in midfield and also take some risks to win the ball a little higher up the field because they have four defenders behind them. This also allows your team to control possession and force your opponent to bring players back toward their goal. This means you can then push your defenders farther up the field. In this situation, if you do lose the ball, you can quickly win it back by pressing the opposition. See Pressing to Get the Ball Back (page 96).

WHERE THERE CAN BE PROBLEMS

The main challenge here is that your team will be very narrow in attacking areas. There are no wingers, so most of the attacking threats will be central, and your single striker will be playing against at least two defenders.

When you do play the ball forward, the timing and selection of the pass is vital. Any mistakes here and the opponents will win the ball back. Even with the right pass at the right time, the two attacking midfielders need to be very mobile and get to a supporting position as soon as possible so your team can keep possession. See Helping The Player With The Ball (page 68).

The last thing to think about is your fullbacks. If they are busy marking the opponent, then they won't be able to get forward. That will leave you outnumbered in your attacking half, making it harder to create scoring chances. Remember, your coach may play this way because your team doesn't score many goals, but this formation could be part of the reason you don't score often.

The 4-2-3-1 and 4-3-2-1 formations are very similar, but the slight changes in how the midfield is lined up make 4-3-2-1 more defensive and easier to play in when you are defending, as you will most likely have more players around the ball. 4-2-3-1 is a little more adventurous when you have the ball, but you must get another player closer to the striker very quickly.

COACH'S CORNER TIPS

Remember to pack two sets of snacks and water in your equipment bag. One is for prep and the second one will help with your recovery as soon as the game ends.

Playing Against a Deep-Lying Block

TYPE OF STRATEGY: Offense attacking

PLAYER TO WATCH: Lionel Messi, player for Barcelona, Paris Saint-Germain, Inter Miami, and Argentina

GAMES TO WATCH: 2022 World Cup games featuring Argentina

Sticking together in a small space can be a good defensive strategy. When a group of defenders stays close to their own goal, we call this a deep-lying block. (See graphic below.) The defenders in that block are referred to as a low block. Teams hang out in their penalty area to block you from scoring, of course.

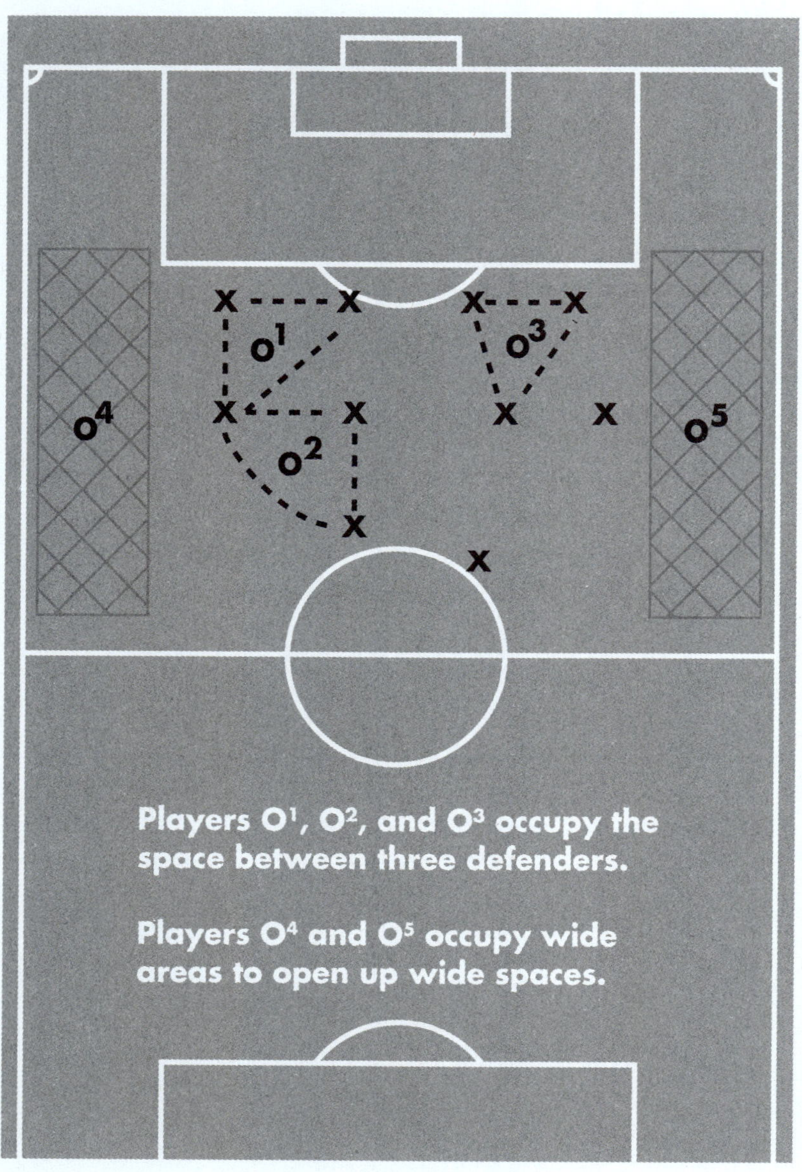
X
X
X
X
O1
X
X
O3
O4
X
X
X
X
O5
O2
X
X
Players O1, O2, and O3 occupy the space between three defenders.
Players O4 and O5 occupy wide areas to open up wide spaces.

TRY IT

When teams sit deep, they concede large areas of the field to the opposition. The way to beat this style of defending is to use every inch of the space they leave open. Wide players must find the spaces that threaten the opponent's fullbacks. If you can get the ball to the wide players, they can create space around the fullbacks. Crisp first-time passing will stretch their back line and make it easier for you to get past them.

Another option is to take long-range shots. If you find yourself in a central position with the ball and some time to look up, I encourage you to let one go from distance. At the threat of a shot, an opponent will come out to close you down, which will create a space for your teammate to fill in; it then offers the teammate room to accept the pass. Quick combination passing can also break down this style of defending. Or, try something out of the ordinary to catch them off guard. Passing across the field all day won't threaten them enough. Use this opportunity to take a few people on and see what that does to their defensive shape. Nothing ventured, nothing gained.

Be patient when faced with this defensive strategy. It only takes a second to score a goal. You will get chances—both chances that you create and chances from their mistakes. Patience is the key to breaking down a deep-lying block.

COACH'S CORNER TIPS

Have a growth mindset. Intelligence and ability can be, and are, developed through your effort, your ability to learn, and most importantly your persistence. You control your ability to improve, so own it!

Playing Against a High Defensive Line

TYPE OF STRATEGY: Offense attacking

PLAYER TO WATCH: Kylian Mbappé, player for Monaco, Paris Saint-Germain, Real Madrid, and France

GAMES TO WATCH: 2018 World Cup games featuring France

PLAYER TO WATCH: Thierry Henry, player for Monaco, Juventus, Arsenal, Barcelona, New York Red Bulls, and France

GAMES TO WATCH: Arsenal (2002–2003)

An opponent's high defensive line, where their back three or back four position themselves, may be as high as just inside their own half. It may sound like it's not as challenging to play against this style of team defending, but when a team plays this way and is well organized, it can be extremely difficult to break them down.

If your opponent is holding a high line, it allows their midfielders to defend higher up the field. That means the midfield group will be closer to their strikers. Can you see where this is going? If your opponents are playing with a back four just inside their half, the remaining six outfield players can be positioned in your half in a compact unit that could be difficult to play through. It is similar to trying to break down a deep-lying opponent, but the big difference is where you are playing. If your opponent sits deep, then you can always go back with the ball if you can't break them down. If you are trying to get out of your own half, though, you may not have the option to go backward if you can break out. The best you might be able to do is play long and get the ball away from your own goal. That is not a great situation to be in.

TRY IT

In order to break down this style of defending, you have to be able to expose the space behind your opponent's back line, and there is a lot of space to expose. It's vital that you challenge your opponent's defensive line at every opportunity. There are a couple of ways that you can do this.

First, whenever you get on the ball, get your hips turned to face your opponent's goal. If they see that you are in space with possession, then a smart back four will drop back to protect the space behind them. Their keeper will also be playing away from the goal line, but far enough to close that space off. As they drop back, so will their midfielders. That does two things: It gives your strikers more room to play in, and it most likely gives you a little more space.

The other things you can do when you are turned around are run at them with the ball or set off on a speed dribble. The opponent must react to what you do, and they will either drop back or hold the line. If they hold the line, then as you get close to the back line, simply play the ball behind them and keep going. If they keep dropping back, at some point you will be in a position to take a shot at goal. The more you disrupt them, the bigger the chance of getting them to play deeper—a tactical win for your team.

COACH'S CORNER TIPS

When things aren't going well ask yourself these questions: What can I do differently to change this and who can help me?

LEVEL

Playing Over, Around, and Through

TYPES OF STRATEGIES: Offense attacking, ball distribution

PLAYER TO WATCH: Andrea Pirlo, player for Brescia, Inter Milan, Reggina, AC Milan, Juventus, New York City FC, and Italy

GAMES TO WATCH: AC Milan (2002–2003), 2006 World Cup games featuring Italy

We talk about playing against teams that sit in a low block, teams that defend with a high line, and teams that use a pressing style of defending. You need to be able to play against multiple styles of play, as well as play over, around, and through your opponents.

If you become a one-dimensional player and rely solely on long passes, for example, teams will learn how to play against you. When you get possession, they will simply drop back and give away space in front of them to take away the area that you are targeting. If you play a lot of cross-field passes or square passes across the field, then the player who is marking you will force you onto your weaker foot or to an area of the field where you can't play that ball across the field. If you are strong at playing through balls for players to run onto, your opponents can block the center of the field and give you passing lanes that lead to wide positions, or they can take away the option by catching your teammates offside.

If you only have one preferred method of play, you will find it difficult to have success. The key is variety and disguise.

TRY IT

There are two types of passes that you should try to avoid if possible: square passes that go horizontal across the field and straight vertical passes that go up the field. A square pass would undo your team if it is intercepted, because you and the person you passed to are now out of position and on the wrong side of the ball. A vertical pass is always a challenge for the person receiving it, because they can't use the angle of the pass to set their body to receive it, and the person playing against them is able to get into a good defensive position directly behind them. When you pass the ball, do everything you can to get an angled pass to your teammate, whether the ball is going forward or you are passing the ball back. Diagonal passes behind your opponent give players an opportunity to catch the ball rather than chase the **straight pass**.

Alongside perfecting diagonal passes, spend some time working on disguising your passes. Watch basketball players execute the no-look pass and try that in games. Once you develop this skill, you'll become a bigger threat to the opponent and a bigger asset to your team.

The last piece of the puzzle is to take all the turns and types of passes we talk about in this book and mix them up to become the most creative player you can be. Don't be afraid of mistakes. View them as learning opportunities.

COACH'S CORNER TIPS

Before you leave the field after a game or a training session, take a minimum of ten minutes to properly cool down both physically and mentally. This will help you recover faster and decrease the chance of injury.

LEVEL ① ② ❸

Long-Distance Passing

TYPE OF TECHNIQUE: Passing, ball striking

PLAYER TO WATCH: Lindsay Heaps (née Horan), player for Colorado Rush, Paris Saint-Germain, Portland Thorns, Lyon, and the United States

GAMES TO WATCH: Paris Saint-Germain (2012–2016); Lyon in the 2022–2025 Women's Champions League knockout stages

PLAYER TO WATCH: Steven Gerrard, player for Liverpool, LA Galaxy, and England

GAMES TO WATCH: Liverpool (2008–2009)

When a long-range pass is executed well, it changes the picture of the game. It enables your team to do a number of things that will increase your chances of creating opportunities. For one, it allows you to switch the point of attack, possibly moving the ball the width of the field in an attempt to unbalance your opponent. It can also create opportunities behind the opponent's defensive line, which is their most vulnerable area. If you can successfully hit this type of pass, your opponent will have to drop back toward their goal and play with a much deeper back line. This creates more space in the midfield, which will give you more time on the ball and more goal-scoring chances.

At the same time, a poorly executed pass can hurt your team. If the pass that is meant to go behind the opponent's back line is under hit and intercepted, then you are under pressure with your teammates on the wrong side of the ball, and they will find it tough to get back into a defensive position. A poorly hit cross-field ball can lead to your team getting caught on a fast break with little cover, so it's important to make sure you have the technique to make this pass before you attempt it.

TRY IT

You'll see this technique when there is a goal kick played into the middle of the field, and sometimes from free kicks in your own half when you want to get the ball high. Very often, this technique demands that the ball be played in the air. You'll also see this type of ball striking in long-range shooting; after all, a shot is a controlled pass to the opponent's goal! With this type of pass, the first thing you need to focus on is the position of the non-kicking foot. It needs to be as far away from the ball as possible, while still allowing you to strike through the center of the ball without losing balance. Once you have this figured out, you can work on the backswing to make sure you have the power you need.

Your non-kicking foot's ankle should be planted slightly ahead of the ball so that on contact you still have power, because your kicking foot is still driving down to the ball. On contact, your ankle is locked and you are striking with your instep, toes down. If you want the ball to go in the air, strike the ball just under the center line and lean back on contact. If you want the ball to stay low, strike through the center of the ball and lean slightly forward on contact.

COACH'S CORNER TIPS

When things are going well, ask yourself this question: What is the next challenge? Always be thinking about how to get better. Don't get comfortable after a little success.

LEVEL

Corners

TYPE OF TECHNIQUE: Attacking, ball striking

PLAYER TO WATCH: Bruno Fernandes, player for Novara, Udinese, Sampdoria, Sporting, Manchester United, and Portugal

GAMES TO WATCH: Manchester United (2020–2021); Portugal in the 2024 Euro Qualification and the 2024–2025 European Nations League

"Inswinger" and "outswinger" are two kinds of corner kicks. Those terms describe the flight of the ball. The direction the ball flies is decided by whether you kick with your right or left foot and whether you take the kick from the left or right side of the field.

If you are right-footed and take a corner from your team's left side, the ball will most likely swing in toward the goal: an inswinger. Right-footed kickers on the right side tend to kick an outswinger. If a left-footed player takes a corner from the left, the ball usually swings out from the goal: an outswinger. Coming from the right, a left-footed player will likely hit an inswinger. See Bending the Ball: Inside of Foot (page 50) for how to practice this technique.

TRY IT

In general, there are two types of delivery. If the ball is driven fast with lower trajectory, or "at pace," we might call it a flat ball. See Long-Distance Passing (page 148). This is difficult to defend; the ball is moving so fast that there is less time for the keeper to decide whether to come and get it or stay on their line.

The other type of delivery is when the ball goes higher up in the air into the danger area and looks like it is hanging in the air. See Chipping the Ball (page 162). This style of corner is really

useful if your team has a couple of players that are good at heading the ball and have good enough timing to start their run from the edge of the penalty area and come onto the ball.

Your focus should be on good delivery, which comes from good technique. Make sure that you place the ball where you want it so that you can get a smooth approach. The more corners you take, the more accurate you will become. If you can hit twenty to thirty extra ones after practice, then you will see a great improvement.

There are many variations of corners, and each team you play will have their own signals to let teammates on the field know what delivery to expect. Learn those signals and perfect your delivery.

As you get older, corners will become more important as they provide a chance to deliver the ball into a dangerous area with no pressure on the ball. They also give your team a chance to play a short corner and keep possession deep in your opponent's half. If you are able to deliver a good corner, then you will be a great asset to your team.

COACH'S CORNER TIPS

We all want to be successful, but if we fail, what will really happen? Failing is part of the process. Fail and then fail better and you will get closer to success. Don't see failure as a negative; always be ready for the next opportunity.

It's a *Foreheader*, Not a *Header*: Safe Heading

There has been an increase in awareness of concussions related to heading the ball. We now know that repetitive heading is linked to brain injury. I can tell you from personal experience that heading the ball incorrectly does and will lead to a concussion. Heading is still a part of soccer, though, so you need to learn how to head the ball correctly.

First off, they should be called forehead-ers because that's where you hit ball—not with the top of your head! Just like using the biggest surface of your foot to get the best accuracy when kicking the ball, the best way to get accuracy when heading the ball is to use the biggest surface of your head: your forehead. It's much safer than the top of your head, too.

Second, don't think of it as a hard hit. It's either a deflection or a touch, really. To add *oomph*, don't rely on your neck muscles. Put your whole body into it to add power, starting with your jump up toward the ball.

Last, since there are different kinds of headers (flick-on passes, header shots on goal, and defending away from goal), there are different types of approach, which I will cover in the next three sections.

Headers: The Flick-On Pass

LEVEL ① ❷ ③

TYPES OF TECHNIQUES: Attacking, modified passing

PLAYER TO WATCH: Peter Crouch, player for Tottenham Hotspur, Queens Park Rangers, Portsmouth, Aston Villa, Southampton, Liverpool, Stoke City, Burnley, and England

GAMES TO WATCH: England (2005–2010), Liverpool (2005–2008), and Stoke City (2011–2019)

When you deflect with a header on a ball coming down from the air, which is called flicking it on, you are trying to change where the ball will land. This action happens a lot at corners, particularly at near post corners. It also happens in the middle area of the **pitch** when you are trying to move the ball forward and are facing your own goal.

Heading flick-ons is a great tactic from a corner, because it quickly changes the flight of the ball when the ball is close to the goal. The keeper and defenders may have done a good job of figuring out where the newly kicked ball is going to land, but a flick from the near post area changes everything! If your team knows the header is planned and gets into place, the other team will be so focused on attacking a different space that the ball can be flicked into an unguarded part of the goal or to an unguarded teammate. Cool move, right?

TRY IT

Before talking about what you want to do, let's make it clear what you *aren't* doing. You are not using the top of your head to flick the ball on. That's not the correct way to head a ball. So how do you flick it the right way?

As the ball comes toward you, position your head with your chin a little higher than normal so your *forehead* (and not the top of your head) will be making contact with the bottom half of the ball. On contact, raise your chin a little more so that your forehead comes up to protect the top of your head. All you are trying to do is flick it on, so you need the lightest of touches.

To flick the ball on to the left or right, twist your head in the direction you want the ball to go just as you are raising your chin. Ensure that when you make contact with the ball it is with your forehead and not the side of your head where the temple is! Stand in the penalty area and have a partner toss the ball in high from the corner area. Practice the light touch of flick-on eight times on one side and eight times on the other. Then take a break. Heading is a skill, and all skills need to be practiced; the difference with heading is that you need to make sure you limit your repetitions to avoid any long-term harm.

COACH'S CORNER TIPS

Make sure that when you practice on your own you balance the things you are working on instead of focusing on one thing for too long. This will keep your mind and body fresh. We learn better when we practice a variety of skills.

LEVEL ① ❷ ③

Headers: Straight into the Goal

TYPES OF TECHNIQUES: Attacking, heading

PLAYER TO WATCH: Ruud Gullit, player for Haarlem, Feyenoord, PSV Eindhoven, AC Milan, Sampdoria, Chelsea, and the Netherlands

GAME TO WATCH: 1988 Euro Final, Netherlands vs. Soviet Union

PLAYER TO WATCH: Abby Wambach, player for Washington Freedom, Ajax, magicJack, Western New York Flash, and the United States

GAME TO WATCH: 2011 Women's World Cup, USA vs. Brazil

In recent years, the trend in the game has been to keep the ball on the ground. Many teams now favor attacks through the center of the pitch, rather than getting the ball out to wide players and asking them to then cross the ball into the 18-yard box for teammates to head into the goal. Even though we are seeing less heading than twenty or thirty years ago, there are still a good percentage of goals scored from it.

When it comes to attacking headers, the keys are being intentional about getting to the ball before the defender, heading the ball down toward the ground, and, if possible, heading the ball back in the direction it came from to throw the keeper off guard.

TRY IT

As the ball is in the air, it's important that you have your eyes on it to figure out its "flight" in order to predict where it's going and at what height it will be when it gets there. The key is to try and get your hips to face the ball, so that when you move to it, you can use your body to generate power in the header. If you want to beat the keeper, you will need some good power in the header, and in general you can't get all that power from just your neck

muscles. You don't want to, either. Stay on your toes, and when you make the decision to attack the ball, make sure you don't grab or pull a defender. The last thing you want is a goal disallowed for a foul.

Make contact with the center line of the ball and try to get the ball moving in a downward direction toward the ground. It can never go too low. Just as with shooting, no one ever headed the ball under the goal. Try to make yourself as tall as possible in the approach to the ball, with your shoulders up and chest open. Right before contact, bring your head down to the ball to direct it toward the ground and into the goal. You should already know where the goal line is. Remember, you are using your forehead, not the top of your head to do this.

The goalkeeper will be moving across the frame of the goal and tracking the ball's movement. Try to head the ball back in the direction it came from, because the keeper will find it very difficult to reverse direction. Combine this with the ball moving toward the ground, and now the keeper is in trouble. They were looking up and in one direction while you were heading it down and in the other direction.

COACH'S CORNER TIPS

When you are practicing headers, make sure the focus of that practice is safety. We learn by repeating, but when it comes to heading, you need to set a limit of six to eight headers per training session. This number may get higher as you get older, but for now, six to eight is the way to go.

★

Headers: On the Defense

LEVEL ① ❷ ③

TYPE OF TECHNIQUE: Defending, heading

PLAYER TO WATCH: Sergio Ramos, player for Sevilla, Real Madrid, Paris Saint-Germain, Monterrey, and Spain

GAME TO WATCH: 2014 Champions League Final, Madrid vs. Atlético

Around 15 to 18 percent of goals are scored from headers. If you can become a player who is strong when it comes to heading the ball in your own defensive area, you could help your team prevent 15 percent of goals on your own. Now, that is a stat that you would want to tell people about!

There are two different types of defensive headers. The first one is simply getting to the ball first to make the first contact. The second is a defensive clearing header. When heading defensively, you want to try to get the ball either out of play as soon as you can so you can regroup, or high and away so you can clear your lines and buy some time and space.

TRY IT

Let's look at a defensive header in which you are marking a player in and around your goal. Focus on staying balanced, and try to be in a position where you can see both the ball being delivered and the player you are directly up against. As the ball comes to you, make sure your hands are out of the way and down by your sides. Any contact from ball to hand will be a penalty if it's inside the 18. Having your hands by your sides will also stop you from pulling or grabbing the attacker, which can also result in a penalty. As you attack the ball, try to get your body in a position where your shoulders are not facing your goal. This isn't always easy, but if you can do this, it will help you deflect

the ball away. I use the word "deflect" as that is how I want you think about this: You are simply trying to get to the ball first so that you can get it away from your goal and away from danger. Again, remember to contact the ball with your forehead, not the top of your head.

COACH'S CORNER TIPS

In training or in games, always focus on getting better. All top-class athletes have failed at times, but they are able to stay focused on their process and the ultimate goal, which is to improve. Stay focused and keep looking ahead.

Drill Downs

Here are some activities that you can do yourself to improve your skills, but make sure you use an appropriate size ball. If you are eight to twelve years old, you are probably still playing with a size 4 ball or smaller, so practice these skills with the ball you're using. As you grow you can move to the full-size ball.

1v1 Against the Keeper

PRACTICE BY YOURSELF

Start on the back of the center circle, facing the nearest goal, about forty-five yards from goal. Push the ball ten yards out. Sprint after the ball and take a shot from around the edge of the penalty box. There is no keeper here, so you need to focus on the posts and crossbar to guide you. Work on matching your speed and stride with the ball, creating an angle to shoot on, and keeping your head up all the way. You know where the ball is; be looking at where you want it to go. Find a comfortable running pace or dribble pattern that allows you to confidently shoot without breaking stride. When you shoot, breathe out to keep the power in your shot; breathing out also makes you more relaxed. If you're stressed when you shoot, it will affect the placement.

Attacking Heading

PRACTICE WITH A PARTNER

BEFORE YOU START: When practicing this drill use a softer ball. There is no need to use a normal ball as you are practicing the technique of heading.

Start on the penalty spot, with your partner behind the goal. Ask your partner to take a throw-in toward you from three to four yards behind the goal, over the crossbars. Focus on the flight of the ball. You want to head the ball *down* into the goal (using your forehead, remember, not the top of your head). Heading it over the knee makes it too easy for the goalkeeper to stop. After eight to ten headers, take a break. Then position yourself on the edge of the goal box (also called the six-yard box), between the corner of the box and the penalty spot. Get your partner to move and take throw-ins from there. Take up to 4 more throw-ins. Repeat from the other side, always aiming for low inside the goal. You're bound to find that you have one side stronger than the other. You never know where the ball will come from; this is why it's such a good drill. After all these practice headers you will need a break. Limit your headers to no more than eight per training session.

Defensive Heading

PRACTICE WITH A PARTNER

BEFORE YOU START: When practicing this drill use a softer ball. There is no need to use a normal ball as you are practicing the technique of heading.

Stand near the goal where you'd normally be if you were defending during the game and were preparing for the other team to make a long cross. Have your partner take a throw-in toward the goal, landing between the edge of the penalty box and the penalty spot. Your job is to judge the ball and clear it with your head (well, your forehead). Repeat four times, then ask your partner to switch sides of the field. This way you get to clear the ball from different angles. After each set of four, take a break. Ask your partner to vary the speed and placement of the throw-in to challenge you even more. Limit your headers to no more than eight for each person

Free Kicks

PRACTICE WITH A PARTNER

Place ten balls around the edge of the penalty box in shooting position. Put your partner on the line by the side of the post, and get them to raise their hands or hold up a target. A plastic trash can lid would be ideal. Have them hold it as high as they can, just under the crossbar. Focus on trying to hit the target. Remember that you also have to get the ball up and over a wall of defenders. As you get better at hitting the high target, slowly increase your power. Once you hit fifteen targets, switch and let your partner take shots while you hold the target. You should aim for forty attempted shots per session, and in time try to build up to a hundred. (Yes, a hundred! You don't get better without hard work.)

Long-Range Shooting

PRACTICE WITH A PARTNER

The drill here is to practice shooting the ball from increasingly farther spots on the field. Line three cones every five yards from the goal, ending thirty yards out. Start by standing at the twenty-five-yard line. Place your partner at the goal line with around ten balls, getting ready to pass them one at a time. On the first pass, strike the ball when it crosses the cone at the twenty-yard line. Hit twenty balls from this point. Use the cones in front of you to judge distance. Can you get them to go farther? Now strike the ball when it passes the cone at twenty-five yards from the goal. Hit another twenty balls from there. How is your accuracy? What do you need to adjust? Finally, try to hit the ball as it passes the thirty-yard line. Remember: Power is nothing without control.

Chipping the Ball

PRACTICE WITH A PARTNER

Your partner will act as goalkeeper, starting on the goal line. Start twenty-five yards out with the ball. Have your partner leave the line and touch the end of the goalkeeper box (six yards from goal) with their hand. As they touch the ground, try to chip the ball over them into the goal. Strike the ball while standing the first time, and then progress to having a touch on the ball before your chip. Try it over and over. As you get better and want a more challenging drill, let the keeper touch the edge of the goalkeeper box (six-yard box) with their foot and try to chip it over their head. When you are consistent at twenty-five yards, move the ball to twenty yards out.

Running with the Ball

PRACTICE THIS BY YOURSELF

Set up a line of eight cones every five yards for thirty-five yards. Starting from the end, run alongside the cones with the ball. Your goal is to have between four and six touches from end to end. Note that this is a running drill. You need to be moving at a good pace, so make sure that after every run you take at least thirty to forty-five seconds to recover. The more runs you do, the longer your recovery needs to be. Try to do eight runs as close to game pace as possible. There is also a conditioning element to this, so as you feel more comfortable with running and recovery, you can try this ten to twelve times.

Juggling

PRACTICE THIS BY YOURSELF

Start juggling with your feet. Create patterns to follow, such as right foot, right thigh, forehead, left thigh, left foot. Now try to work that pattern through and back again to finish on your left foot. How many times can you complete a circuit before the ball hits the ground? Now create a pattern that includes both feet, both thighs, your forehead, and your chest. Try that same pattern and back again. Challenge yourself, but don't count your touches. Don't look to compete with teammates. What matters is that you can control the ball and not be controlled by the ball.

Ball Manipulation

PRACTICE THIS BY YOURSELF

Look at your feet. The outside of your left foot is Area 1, the inside of your left foot is Area 2, the inside of your right foot is Area 3, and the outside of your right foot is Area 4. Now, in a 15-by-20-yard rectangle (about half the penalty area), start dribbling the ball up and down in this specific pattern: 1-2-3-4. Once you have that mastered, try 1-2-3-4-4-3-2-1. Work on keeping your head up as often as possible. You know where your feet are!

This can be tricky to start with; you need to let your feet and brain get coordinated. Take your time, start slowly, and increase your speed when you are ready.

Half Volleys

PRACTICE THIS BY YOURSELF OR WITH A PARTNER

On the edge of the 18-penalty area, build two 10-by-10-yard boxes going away from the goal. You now have two squares. Start at the back square and juggle the ball through the boxes. The ball can bounce on the ground, but only once in each box. When you get to the edge of the 18, pop the ball up to head height, let it bounce, and then strike a half volley. When you have mastered the technique, add a keeper.

For Parents

Understanding the Developmental Process

You play a vital role in your child's enjoyment of soccer by being the best Integrated Support Team.

One of the things to be aware of for this age group is the developmental process and how it can have different effects on different children. In this section I will talk about **Relative Age Effect** (RAE) and **early maturation**. Relative Age Effect relates to when your child is born. Early maturation creates challenges in the sport system. I want to make it clear that we can't change either. What we can do is understand them, accept them, and support our children.

The theory of Relative Age Effect states that at the high-performance level, on average, athletes born earlier in the year are more likely to be successful. Some people refer to RAE as the 40-30-20-10 rule because the research that has been carried out shows the following: 40 percent of high-performance athletes are likely to be born in the first quarter of the year—January, February, and March; 30 percent are likely to be born in the second quarter of the year; 20 percent are likely to be born in the third quarter; and 10 percent of high-performance athletes are born in the last quarter of the year—October, November, and December.

One of the main reasons for this theory is the way we structure soccer teams and leagues. Because of the number of players involved, there has to be a clear and simple way to form teams, and that is by birth year. The simplest cut-off dates are January 1 to December 31. That means that a child born in late December will play with and against players born in January and will be up to twelve months younger than some players. If you are in your midtwenties, this isn't that big of a deal. But if you are ten years old this can be a huge challenge in terms of body size and body weight.

Early maturation also poses problems for many athletes in the developmental stages. As a parent you know that no two children are the same. They develop at different times and at different rates, and the development process doesn't go at one steady speed. If a child starts to go through growth spurts earlier, then they will be a little faster and a little stronger, and sometimes, but not always, a little more coordinated. As you can imagine, this will be a real help to that particular child, but at the expense of others.

As a coach, one of the problems I see with early maturation is that it is often mistaken for talent. The bigger, faster, and stronger kids will stand out as they mature, and very often these players make the team over the players who have not yet started the development process. When players are selected to teams, their confidence grows. When we don't get selected, our confidence takes a hit, and believe me when I tell you I know how this feels.

We cannot change how our children grow, nor should we, and we probably can't make a wholesale change to how we select soccer teams. But there are some things that you can do to support your child.

The first thing you can do is talk about this with your soccer player and help them understand that this is just a part of the journey. Relative Age Effect and early maturation don't always favor those who benefit from them in the long run.

Soccer is a highly technical game, and it's the *technical ability* of a soccer player that counts. If it was all about physicality, speed, and strength, then all players would be tall, have Olympic speed, and have the strength of a weightlifter. Lionel Messi does not fit that profile—he is five feet seven inches tall!

If your child benefits from either RAE or early maturation, or both, then it's really important that they continue to practice their techniques. They can't always rely on being faster and stronger. This happens to many players who are selected early. They don't improve their skills, and other players catch them up to them physically and then pass them technically.

If your child is born later in the year or is a late developer, the first thing to do is reassure them it's perfectly normal. These players need to work hard on their technique, and if they really want to go far, they must take full advantage of good nutrition and adequate sleep, and learn as much as they can from their coach. Many coaches understand the challenges that RAE and the maturation process cause, and *all* coaches want to work with inquisitive and hungry athletes.

Glossary

ahead of the ball (also called above the ball or past the ball) The area closer to the opponent's goal than the ball when your team is in possession. In contrast, "below the ball" is the area closer to your goal than the ball when your team is in possession.

back four Four teammates playing defense, placed closest to their goal. It's usually two central defenders and two fullbacks.

ball manipulation Using different parts of your feet to move the ball around

basketball pick Play where the defender is blocked by an offensive player who stands still and doesn't move, so their teammate can pass by. Sometimes this will be called as a foul.

block In addition to preventing the ball from going forward, the term "block" means a group of players organized to defend a space. A "low block" is a group of defenders near their goal trying to prevent the other team from scoring.

cues Things you notice in the game that tell you what will likely happen next. For example, if the other team tries to play a long ball (make a long pass) behind your back four (defense), that is a cue for your team to drop back (head to your goal and start defending).

early maturation When a person starts puberty earlier than their peers

far post The post farthest away from the ball. This changes whenever the ball goes across the field.

FIFA (Fédération Internationale de Football Association) The world's governing body for soccer

flick it on When a player deflects with a header on a ball that's coming down from the air

front foot The foot closest to the opponent's goal

higher up the field Moving up the field toward the opponent's goal, where you want to score

inside The area toward the center of the field, away from the sidelines

Integrated Support Team (IST) A group of physiologists, dietitians, athletic therapists, mental performance consultants, and other professionals who support athletes

near post The post closest to the ball. This changes whenever the ball goes across the field.

on an angle A shot, pass, or supporting position on a diagonal line from the ball

outside The area toward the nearest sideline

pitch The playing surface of the game; also known as the soccer field

plant foot The non-kicking foot

pressing A style of defending that puts pressure on the ball carrier. This is not a style of play. Can be incorporated into any team formation or structure.

Relative Age Effect (RAE) Describes how difference in birth month can create advantages and disadvantages for athletes who play sports in a system grouped by birth years

second six The area between the six-yard line and the penalty spot that is the same width as the six-yard box

square position or square pass On a horizontal line across the field, such as across the halfway line

straight pass A pass on a vertical line up or down the field, such as down the sidelines

the 18 The penalty area, or penalty box, which is a rectangle, 18 yards to each side of the goal line and 18 yards in front of it

thirds of the field The field is divided into thirds: the **defending/bottom third** in front of your goal, the **middle third** where you'll likely find midfielders, and the **top/attacking third** where your team will be trying to score.

Union of European Football Associations (UEFA) The governing body for soccer in Europe

Resources

WEBSITES

The Equalizer: One of the best sources for news and views on women's soccer. Follow your favorite players overseas and in the United States. Learn about the different clubs in European women's soccer. Pick a team to follow in every country!
EqualizerSoccer.com

TNT Sports: Keeps you up-to-date with all the goings-on in European soccer, from the Premier League to Scottish football. Includes a running tally of recent game scores and links to European articles about players, coaches, and games.
TNTSports.co.uk/football

Major League Soccer: All the news and happenings in the world of Major League Soccer. This website gives you all the news from the MLS and helps you stay informed on game results, player trades, and up-and-coming young players to watch.
MLSSoccer.com

United States Youth Soccer Association: Information on soccer programming across the United States, including soccer news, social events, and tournaments. Get the latest on what's happening in clubs in every state. *USYouthSoccer.org*

National Women's Soccer League: Everything you need to know about the premier women's soccer league in the U.S.
NWSLSoccer.com

Index

E

F

G

H

I

J

S

T

U

V

W

X

Y

Z

Acknowledgments

To the best team, the home team, my family: Joanne, Hope, Ollie, Jake, Lawrence, and Sheldon. Family isn't everything—it's the only thing.

Many years ago, a great coach, Roy Rees, turned on a light in my brain and it continues to burn bright. Over the years, many colleagues have helped keep that light on; there isn't enough room to name you all, but you know who you are.

About the Author

Andrew Latham has been involved in soccer coaching for over thirty years, working with athletes and coaches in North America and the United Kingdom, including three years with Sheffield United, where he played a key role in introducing futsal to the Academy players.

He holds numerous coaching licenses in North America and the UK and has been a coach developer in British Columbia for over twenty years. He is a graduate of the National Institute of Canada and has a master's degree in Coaching Education from the University of Victoria.

He is currently the Manager of Performance Pathways for the Canadian Sport Institute Pacific. He is responsible for coach and athlete education and supporting the provincial sport organizations of British Columbia as their athletes strive to represent Canada at the highest levels.

Notes on My Performance